EXPLORING
ENGLISH

6

Tim Harris • Allan Rowe

Longman

Exploring English 6

Copyright © 1997 by Addison Wesley Longman
All rights reserved.

Text credit: page 164, TV-Free America

Pearson Education, 10 Banks Street, White Plains, NY 10606

Editorial Director: Joanne Dresner
Acquisitions Editor: Anne Boynton-Trigg
Production Editor: Liza Pleva
Text Design: Curt Belshe, Naomi Ganor
Cover Design: Curt Belshe
Cover Illustration: Allan Rowe
Electronic Production Supervisor: Kim Teixeira
Composition: Kathleen Marks

Library of Congress Cataloging-in-Publication Data
Harris, Tim
    Exploring English / Tim Harris; illustrated by Allan Rowe.
      p.   cm.
ISBN 0-201-82588-0
    1. English language—Textbooks for foreign speakers. I. Rowe,
Allan. II. Title.
PE1128.H347 1997
428.2'4—dc20   94-47408
                                        CIP

       7 8 9 10-CRK-01

To our families

Contents

Chapter 5   80

TOPICS
Adventure
Travel

GRAMMAR
Third conditional
Perfect modals

FUNCTIONS
Expressing past advisability
Expressing regret
Expressing possibility in the past
Making logical conclusions
Giving opinions

Chapter 6   101

TOPICS
Your family history
Music
Success
Jobs

GRAMMAR
Future continuous
Future perfect
Uses of "get" (review)

FUNCTIONS
Talking about the future
Communicating without words
Making predictions
Giving opinions

Chapter 7   127

TOPICS
Politics
Current issues
Health
Love, faith, and miracles

GRAMMAR
Participles

FUNCTIONS
Describing a series of actions
Making complaints
Summarizing conversations
Asking for and giving information

Chapter 8   152

TOPICS
American holidays
Proverbs
Television
Lying

GRAMMAR
Review

FUNCTIONS
Expressing possibility and probability
Saying good-bye
Making recommendations
Agreeing and disagreeing

Appendix   172

Irregular verbs
Participles used as adjectives
Phrasal verbs
Gerunds and infinitives
Tapescripts

Preface

Exploring English is a comprehensive, six-level course for adult and young adult students of English. It teaches all four language skills—listening, speaking, reading, and writing—with an emphasis on oral communication. The course combines a strong grammar base with in-depth coverage of language functions and life skills.

Exploring English:

Teaches grammar inductively. The basic structures are introduced in context through illustrated situations and dialogues. Students use the structures in talking about the situations and re-enacting the dialogues. They encounter each structure in a variety of contexts, including practice exercises, pair work activities, and readings. This repeated exposure enables students to make reliable and useful generalizations about the language. They develop a "language sense"—a feeling for words—that carries over into their daily use of English.

Includes language functions in every chapter from beginning through advanced levels. Guided conversations, discussions, and role plays provide varied opportunities to practice asking for and giving information, expressing likes and dislikes, agreeing and disagreeing, and so on.

Develops life skills in the areas most important to students: food, clothing, transportation, work, housing, and health care. Everyday life situations provide contexts for learning basic competencies: asking directions, taking a bus, buying food, shopping for clothes, and so on. Students progress from simpler tasks, such as describing occupations at the beginning level, to interviewing for jobs and discussing problems at work at more advanced levels.

Incorporates problem solving and critical thinking in many of the lessons, especially at the intermediate and advanced levels. The stories in *Exploring English* present a cast of colorful characters who get involved in all kinds of life problems, ranging from personal relationships to work-related issues and politics. Students develop critical-thinking skills as they discuss these problems, give their opinions, and try to find solutions. These discussions also provide many opportunities for students to talk about their own lives.

Provides extensive practice in listening comprehension through illustrated situations. Students are asked to describe each illustration in their own words before listening to the accompanying story (which appears on the reverse side of the page). Then they answer questions based on the story, while looking at the illustration. The students respond to what they see and hear without referring to a text, just as they would in actual conversation.

Offers students frequent opportunities for personal expression. The emphasis throughout *Exploring English* is on communication—encouraging students to use the language to express their own ideas and feelings. Free-response questions in

Books 1 and 2 give students the opportunity to talk about themselves using simple, straightforward English. Every chapter in Books 3–6 has a special section, called "One Step Further," that includes discussion topics such as work, leisure activities, cinema, travel, dating, and marriage. Ideas for role plays are also provided to give additional opportunities for free expression. The general themes are familiar to students because they draw on material already covered in the same chapter. Role plays give students a chance to interact spontaneously— perhaps the most important level of practice in developing communication skills.

Provides continuous review and reinforcement. Each chapter concludes with a review section, and every fourth chapter is devoted entirely to review, allowing students to practice newly acquired language in different combinations.

Presents attractive art that visually supports and is integral with the language being taught. Humorous and imaginative illustrations, in full color, make *Exploring English* fun for students. In addition, the richness of the art allows teachers to devise their own spin-off activities, increasing the teachability of each page.

Each level of *Exploring English* is accompanied by a Workbook. The Workbook lessons are closely coordinated with the lessons in the Student Book. They provide additional writing practice using the same grammatical structures and vocabulary while expanding on basic functions and life skills. The activities range from sentence-completion exercises to guided paragraph and composition writing.

Student Books and Workbooks include clear labels and directions for each activity. In addition, Teacher's Resource Manuals are available for each level. These Manuals provide step-by-step guidance for teaching each page, expansion activities, and answers to the exercises. For levels 1–4, each student page is reproduced for easy reference.

Audiocassettes for each level featuring an entertaining variety of native voices round out the series.

Cast of Characters

Here are the people you will be reading about. They live in Wickam City.

Mr. Bascomb, rich and powerful, is running for mayor of Wickam City. He is pro-business and wants to build a toy factory in City Park.

Otis Jackson, an artist, is also running for mayor of Wickam City. He is very concerned about the environment and wants to save City Park for the people.

Anne Jones is a secretary at City Bank. She is bored with her job and dreams of becoming a professional singer.

Johnnie Wilson is the owner of Johnnie's Bookstore. He is in love with Anne, but afraid to tell her how he feels.

Barbara Martinoli is one of Anne's friends and a co-worker at City Bank. She is married to Tino Martinoli.

Tino Martinoli, Barbara's husband, works as a waiter in his father's Italian restaurant. He dreams of going to Italy some day.

Maria Miranda is a young doctor who is very popular with her patients at Frampton Hospital.

Peter Smith is a successful businessman. He is also a world traveler who loves adventure.

Marty Mango, 10, is a student at Wickam Elementary School. He has been having a hard time since his father died.

Fred Farmer is a former professional baseball player. He tries to help boys like Marty who come from poor families.

Barney Field is a taxi driver. He and Fred are best friends.

Suzi Suzuki, star reporter for the Wickam Daily News, always covers the big stories.

Nancy Paine is a pilot. She is very brave, often risking her life to help people in emergency situations.

Dr. Pasto is a highly respected professor. Many people go to him for advice when they are having personal problems.

Chapter 1

1. *Talk about the pictures.*
2. *Listen to the story.*
3. *Answer the story questions.*

Mr. Bascomb was upset. At times like this he wished he had never become a candidate for mayor. Everything had gone wrong that morning. Even before leaving the house he had received a telephone call from his campaign manager asking for money. Mr. Bascomb had no volunteers, and the people working for him refused to do any more work until they were paid. This made him angry and he left the house in a bad mood.

When Mr. Bascomb arrived at the office, he realized that he had left his briefcase at home. He tried calling his wife, but the line was busy. She was always talking on the phone, and this annoyed Mr. Bascomb a great deal. He could feel his head pounding. He reached for the aspirin, but the bottle was empty. He had forgotten to pick up some aspirin at the drugstore.

Mr. Bascomb looked at his watch. He was to deliver a campaign speech at the Founders' Club at eleven o'clock. He had given a rough draft of his speech to Barbara the day before and asked her to type it up for him. He hadn't seen her when he came into the office and now he was very worried. Just then the telephone rang. It was Barbara. She explained that she had had a flat tire and couldn't be at work until twelve o'clock.

Mr. Bascomb was desperate. He didn't know what to do. He finally called Anne into his office and tried dictating his speech from memory. But it was hopeless. Anne couldn't type a single line without making a mistake. Mr. Bascomb wished that he had never hired her. He finally left the room to keep from losing his temper.

Mr. Bascomb was very nervous when he arrived at the Founders' Club. He couldn't remember anything he had planned to say to his audience. He started talking about himself and his problems instead of talking about the problems of Wickam City. Most of the people in the audience were bored. By the time Mr. Bascomb finished his speech, almost everyone had fallen asleep or left the room. No one came up afterward to shake his hand or wish him well. Mr. Bascomb was very disappointed. He decided to go home for lunch and tell his wife what had happened.

1. How did Mr. Bascomb feel this morning? Was he happy or upset?
2. Had he received a letter or a telephone call before he left the house?
3. What did his campaign manager ask for?
4. What did Mr. Bascomb realize when he arrived at the office?
5. Why couldn't he talk to his wife on the phone?
6. What had Mr. Bascomb forgotten to pick up at the drugstore?
7. Where was Mr. Bascomb going to deliver a speech?
8. Had he given a rough draft of his speech to Anne or Barbara the day before?
9. Why couldn't Barbara be at work until twelve o'clock?
10. Why was it hopeless for Mr. Bascomb to dictate his speech to Anne?
11. What did he wish about Anne?
12. Why was Mr. Bascomb nervous when he arrived at the Founders' Club?
13. What did he talk about?
14. What had happened by the time Mr. Bascomb finished his speech?
15. What did he decide to do?
16. Have you ever had a day when everything went wrong?

PAST PERFECT

He realized that he had made a mistake.

_____ forgotten something.

_____ left his briefcase at home.

_____ wasted a lot of time.

Past —— X ——————————————— X ————————————— | ———— Future

Now

He left his briefcase at home. He realized his mistake.
He realized that he **had left** his briefcase at home.

We use the past perfect for an action that took place before the time of our thinking or speaking about it. The past perfect is formed with **had** + past participle.

WRITTEN EXERCISE • *Complete the sentences using the past perfect. Then read the sentences aloud.*

Mr. Bascomb realized that he ___*had left*___ his briefcase at home.
(leave)

Barbara explained that she ___*had had*___ a flat tire on the way to work.
(have)

1. Mr. Hamby told us that he _____ hard all his life.
(work)

2. He was disappointed that his wife _____ all their money on new furniture.
(spend)

3. She explained that she _____ everything on sale.
(buy)

4. Barbara felt that she _____ a good tennis player.
(become)

5. She knew that she _____ considerably.
(improve)

6. I heard that she _____ every game against Nancy.
(win)

7. John's report showed that the company _____ 20 percent in one year.
(grow)

8. He thought that all the employees _____ a good job.
(do)

9. I felt that I _____ a lot at the last meeting.
(learn)

10. My boss told me that I _____ a good impression.
(make)

Listen and practice.

MR. BASCOMB: What a terrible morning. I hadn't even finished shaving when my campaign manager called to give me some bad news.

MRS. BASCOMB: You poor dear. You'll feel better as soon as you've had something to eat.

pres perf.

MR. BASCOMB: Not unless your cooking has improved considerably. Henrietta, you wouldn't believe what happened this morning.

MRS. BASCOMB: Dear, you worry too much. You should relax when you come home.

MR. BASCOMB: How can I relax when everything goes wrong? Barbara was supposed to type up my speech and bring it to the office this morning. At ten o'clock she called in saying that she'd had a flat tire.

MRS. BASCOMB: Well, where was Anne?

MR. BASCOMB: Anne. Hah! I tried dictating my speech to her, but she couldn't type a single line without making a mistake. I wish I'd never hired her.

MRS. BASCOMB: Don't be too hard on Anne. I'm sure she wasn't doing it on purpose.

MR. BASCOMB: Oh, if only Barbara had come to work on time. When I got to the Founders' Club I couldn't remember anything I'd planned to say. My speech was a disaster. Almost everyone had fallen asleep or left the room by the time I finished. What a life! I'll never win the election this way.

MRS. BASCOMB:	I understand how you feel, dear. But don't think about it or you'll ruin your lunch. Why, you've hardly touched your chicken and peas.
MR. BASCOMB:	If only you <u>hadn't made</u> chicken and peas. If I've told you once, I've told you a thousand times, I can't stand chicken and peas.
MRS. BASCOMB:	John, you complain too much. Do you know what I wish?
MR. BASCOMB:	No, what?
MRS. BASCOMB:	I wish you <u>hadn't come</u> home for lunch.

WISH + PAST PERFECT

He wishes he hadn't gone to work.

_____ hired Anne Jones.

_____ given such a poor speech.

_____ become a candidate for mayor.

PRACTICE • *Change the sentences using **wish** and the past perfect.*

> Mr. Bascomb is sorry he hired Anne Jones.
> **He wishes he hadn't hired her.**
>
> Anne is sorry she became a secretary.
> **She wishes she hadn't become a secretary.**

1. Mr. Bascomb is sorry he became a candidate for mayor.
2. He's sorry he gave such a poor speech.
3. Anne is sorry she made so many mistakes.
4. She is sorry she wasted so much time.
5. Barbara is sorry she came to work late.
6. Nick is sorry he sold his motorcycle.
7. He's sorry he missed the football game.
8. My sister is sorry she spent all her money.
9. She's sorry she bought so many clothes.

When talking about two actions which happened in the past, use the past perfect for the action which happened first. Use the past tense for the second, more recent action. The past perfect is often used with **because, by the time, as soon as,** and **when.**

> ①　　　　　　　　　　　　　②
> Almost everyone **had left** by the time he **finished** his speech.
>
> ②　　　　　　　　①
> He **was** upset because he **had given** a terrible speech.

Either the past tense or the past perfect is used with **before** and **after.**

> ①
> He **received**　　　　　　　　　　　②
> 　　**had received** a phone call before he **left** the house.
>
> ②　　　　　　　　①
> He **felt** better after he **talked**
> 　　　　　　　　　　**had talked** with his wife.

WRITTEN EXERCISE • *Complete the sentences using the past tense or the past perfect, whichever is more appropriate. Then read the sentences aloud.*

I ___*felt*___ better as soon as I ___*had had*___ something to eat.
(feel)　　　　　　　　　　　　　　　(have)

Maria ___*had lived*___ here less than a year when she ___*met*___ Peter.
(live)　　　　　　　　　　　　　　　　　　　　(meet)

1. As soon as we _____ enough money, we _____ some new
(save)　　　　　　　　　　　　　　(buy)
furniture.

2. I _____ a vacation because I _____ very hard.
(need)　　　　　　　　　　　　(work)

3. Nick _____ how to repair cars by the time he _____ fifteen.
(learn)　　　　　　　　　　　　　　　　　　　(be)

4. He _____ a mechanic for 10 years when he _____ his garage.
(be)　　　　　　　　　　　　　　　　　(open)

5. Albert _____ to Linda's party as soon as he _____ his homework.
(go)　　　　　　　　　　　　　　　　　(finish)

6. He _____ to take a taxi because he _____ the last bus.
(have)　　　　　　　　　　　　　　(miss)

7. Many of the guests _____ by the time Albert _____ at the party.
(leave)　　　　　　　　　　　　　(arrive)

8. Linda _____ upset because Albert _____ so late.
(be)　　　　　　　　　　　　　(come)

WHAT'S HAPPENING HERE?

1. *Talk about the pictures.*
2. *Listen to the story.*
3. *Answer the story questions.*

READING

It was five o'clock in the afternoon. Barney had just had his hair cut at Clancy's Barber Shop and was having his shoes shined when Fred came running up to him. Fred was out of breath and looked worried. He had spent the whole day looking for Marty and he thought Barney could help him find the boy. Marty's mother had tried to make him go to the dentist to have his teeth checked. But Marty was scared and didn't want to go. Now he had disappeared and Fred thought Marty had run away from home.

Barney told Fred that he was going to Nick's Garage to have his car washed and get his tank filled up with gas. Lots of kids from the neighborhood went there because Nick let them play in the old wrecked cars behind the garage. It was possible that one of them had seen Marty or knew where he was. Barney offered to give Fred a ride to the garage in his taxi.

When the two men arrived at Nick's, they found Marty playing with some other boys. Fred convinced Marty that he had to be brave and go to the dentist "like a man." Marty finally agreed, but only if Fred would go there with him to give him courage. Fred smiled and put his arm around Marty. They got in Barney's taxi and went to the dentist together.

1. Where did Barney have his hair cut?
2. What was he doing when Fred came running up to him?
3. Who had Fred been looking for all day?
4. Why couldn't Marty's mother get him to go to the dentist?
5. Where did Fred and Barney find Marty?
6. How did Fred get Marty to go to the dentist?

HAVE SOMETHING DONE

Barney had his hair cut.

_____ shoes shined.

_____ car washed.

_____ tank filled up.

WRITTEN EXERCISE • *Complete the sentences with the past participle of the appropriate verb. Compare with a partner.*

Barney had his hair ____*cut*____.
Nancy had her clothes *laundered*.

1. The Bascombs had their kitchen _____ yellow.

2. Their gate was broken, so they had it _____.

3. Peter had twelve roses _____ to his girlfriend.

4. I like Peter's new suit. He had it _____ in New York.

5. Maria went to the bank to have a check _____.

6. She spent twenty dollars to have her picture _____.

| cash |
| cut |
| deliver |
| launder |
| make |
| paint |
| repair |
| take |

Listen and practice.

MARTY: Gee, Fred, I'm scared! I wish you hadn't made me come.

FRED: Nonsense, Marty. There's nothing to be afraid of. We all have to have our teeth checked once in a while. Why, it's no more frightening than having your eyes examined.

MARTY: Don't you ever get scared, Fred?

FRED: There are a lot of things that scare me, Marty. But there's nothing in the world that can make me run.

DR. MOLAR: Well, well. So we're going to have our teeth checked, are we?

MARTY: I don't want to have anything done. All I want to do is go home. Please, Fred, don't make me stay.

FRED: Now, Marty, I told you there was nothing to worry about. Why once, when I was in the army, I had to get a tooth pulled without any painkiller.

MARTY: Yeah, Fred, but you're brave!

DR. MOLAR: I have an idea, Mr. Farmer. Why don't you sit in the chair and let me check your teeth? That will make the boy feel more confident. Who knows, I might even find a cavity that needs filling.

MARTY: That's a great idea, Fred. I won't be afraid if I see you go first.

FRED: Well, that is . . . I'm not sure . . .

DR. MOLAR: Sit down over here, Mr. Farmer. This will only take a minute.

FRED: Oh . . . I just remembered an urgent appointment. Would you mind letting us come back tomorrow? I've really got to run now.

VERB + OBJECT + INFINITIVE (without "TO")

They made him go to the dentist.
_____ have his teeth checked.
_____ do his homework.
_____ clean his room.

PAIR WORK • *Have conversations similar to the examples.*

| A: **Did Marty want to go to the dentist?** | B: **No, Fred made him go to the dentist.** |
| A: **Did Jenny want to wash the dishes?** | B: **No, her father made her wash the dishes.** |

1. A: Did Tino want to paint the living room? B: No, Barbara _____.
2. A: Did he want to buy a new coffee table? B: No, she _____.
3. A: Did Anne want to work on Saturday? B: No, Mr. Bascomb _____.
4. A: Did she want to clean the office? B: No, he _____.
5. A: Did Marty want to do his homework? B: No, his mother _____.
6. A: Did he want to put away his comic books? B: No, she _____.
7. A: Did Jenny want to turn off the TV? B: No, her parents _____.
8. A: Did she want to go to bed? B: No, they _____.
9. A: Did Fred want to look for a job? B: No, his sister _____.
10. A: Did he want to wear a suit and tie? B: No, she _____.

Dr. Pasto was standing on the front porch of his house. It was a beautiful day. The sun was shining, the birds were singing, and Dr. Pasto was whistling as he watered his flowers. Anne Jones came walking up the sidewalk leading to the porch. She looked nervous and upset.

"Dr. Pasto," she called. "I need to speak to you. Do you have a few minutes?"

"Of course, Anne," replied Dr. Pasto. "I always have time to talk to good friends. Come up and have a nice cold glass of lemonade."

Anne started up the steps. On the way she stumbled and bumped her knee. Then she burst into tears.

"Oh, Dr. Pasto," she cried. "I'm so clumsy and awkward and useless. Sometimes I wish I had never been born."

"Now, Anne," said Dr. Pasto. "We all have our bad moments, but it's a crime to be sad on a day like today. Why don't you tell me your problems? Perhaps I can help you."

Anne's hand was shaking as she accepted a glass of lemonade from Dr. Pasto. It slipped from her hand and fell to the floor. Pieces of glass and ice and drops of lemonade flew everywhere. Anne began to cry even harder. "That's part of the problem, Dr. Pasto," she said. "Everything I touch falls apart or breaks. I can't do anything right."

"Well, Anne," said Dr. Pasto. "Experience has shown me that being clumsy or accident prone is not usually a problem in itself, but a symptom of a deeper problem or difficulty. Now, what is it that's upsetting you, Anne?"

"Well, Dr. Pasto," said Anne, drying her tears. "I can't stand my job. It makes me feel so frustrated. There's never anything interesting to do, and when there is, Mr. Bascomb never lets me do it. He has Barbara do all the important work."

"Can you give me an example, Anne?"

"Yes. Just yesterday, for instance. Mr. Bascomb called me into his office and started dictating a speech he was going to give at the Founders' Club. There was very little time and he kept looking over my shoulder, which made me very uncomfortable. I made a lot of mistakes and Mr. Bascomb got upset with me. He said that I was a lousy secretary. Naturally, I felt terrible, Dr. Pasto. He always makes me do the uninteresting, routine work, and when he finally lets me do something important, I make a mess of it."

"Hmm, I see," said Dr. Pasto. "You're clumsy and you break things because you're nervous, and you're nervous because you're dissatisfied with your job. Is it just Mr. Bascomb you don't like, or don't you like being a secretary?"

"Actually, I guess Mr. Bascomb is all right," replied Anne. "The trouble is with me. I wish I'd never become a secretary."

"Well, some people aren't suited for some jobs, Anne, and it's foolish to go against your nature. Now, tell me, what would you really like to do?"

Anne blushed and hesitated. "Well," she said, "I know it sounds ridiculous, but I'd really like to be a professional singer."

"I see nothing ridiculous in that, Anne," said Dr. Pasto. "I know you have a beautiful voice. The question is, do you have the courage to follow your dream?"

"I don't know, Dr. Pasto. It's such a struggle. I don't even know how to begin."

"Listen, Anne. Nothing in life that is really worthwhile comes easily. If you want to succeed, you have to take risks. Be bold and courageous. When you look back on your life, you'll regret the things you didn't do more than the things you did." Anne nodded silently. Dr. Pasto continued, "I have some friends in Hollywood who are in the entertainment business. I'm sure they'd be happy to arrange an audition for you."

Anne started to smile. "Oh, Dr. Pasto, if only I'd talked to you before. You're so wonderful. I feel my whole life is going to be different from now on. I'm going to give you a big kiss."

Anne was about to throw her arms around Dr. Pasto when she bumped into the table, causing the pitcher of lemonade to fall on the floor and break. Anne looked worried, but Dr. Pasto smiled. "Never mind, Anne. After all, it takes more than a few minutes to change your life."

STORY QUESTIONS

1. Why did Anne go to see Dr. Pasto?
2. What's upsetting Anne?
3. Why is Anne dissatisfied with her job?
4. What would she really like to do?
5. What advice did Dr. Pasto give Anne? Do you agree with him?

FREE RESPONSE

1. Why do some people continue at jobs they don't like?
2. Do you think it's better to take risks in life or to play it safe?
3. When was the last time you took a risk? What happened?
4. What is your dream? What would you really like to do?

CLASS ACTIVITY • *Look at the pictures of Ellen and Robert. Can you guess what they're thinking?*

Ellen

Robert

 LISTENING • *Listen to Ellen and Robert; then answer the questions below.*

- What is Ellen's problem?
- What advice would you give her?

- What is Robert's problem?
- What advice would you give him?

ROLE PLAY • *Student A plays Ellen. Student B plays Robert. Robert finally gets the courage to ask Ellen for a date. She's very surprised.*

1. A: Did Mr. Lassiter let Jenny watch TV?
   B: **No. He made her do her homework.**

2. A: Did the park ranger let Marty and Billy fish in the pond?
   B: **No. He made them leave.**

3. A: Did Mona let Fred sleep late?

4. A: Did Mrs. Stumbo let her boys play in the kitchen?

5. A: Did Johnnie let Ed use his comb?

6. A: Did Mr. Farley let his wife play the radio?

7. A: Did Blossom let Ed eat with his fingers?

8. A: Did Mr. Bascomb let Anne and Barbara take a long coffee break?

9. A: Did Mr. Meany let Candy pay with a credit card?

GROUP WORK • *Think of a time in your life when someone made you do something you didn't want to do. Share your experience with the group.*

FREE RESPONSE 1

1. Should cities let homeless people sleep in parks?
2. Should the government make everyone work?
3. Should companies let their employees wear jeans?
4. Should teachers make their students do homework every day?
5. Should parents let their children watch whatever they want on TV?
6. Should parents make their children help with the housework?
7. Should husbands let their wives be the boss?
8. Should wives let their husbands make the big decisions?

WRITTEN EXERCISE • *Complete the sentences.*

My neighbor pays someone ___*to clean her house.*___
___*to launder her clothes.*___

1. The teacher expects his students _____

2. The doctor advises all of her patients _____

3. The landlord doesn't allow the tenants _____

4. We want the government _____

5. I can't get my sister _____

6. She always tells her husband _____

7. We often invite our friends _____

8. Would you please remind me _____

FREE RESPONSE 2

1. Do you pay to have your hair cut or do you cut it yourself?
2. Do you have your clothes laundered or do you wash them yourself?
3. When was the last time you had your eyes examined?
4. Have you ever had an X-ray taken? When? Where?
5. Have you ever had a dress (suit) (shirt) made?
6. Have you ever had anything stolen from your house? What were the circumstances?

PRACTICE • *In the pictures below, the action on the left precedes the action on the right. Combine the sentences about the people in the pictures using the past perfect.*

1. Almost everyone left the Founders' Club.   Mr. Bascomb finished his speech.

   Almost everyone **had left** the Founders' Club by the time Mr. Bascomb finished his speech.

2. Mario worked as a cook for ten years.   He opened his own restaurant.

   Mario **had worked** as a cook for ten years by the time he opened his own restaurant.

3. Sam got dressed.   Mable woke up.

4. Peter went home.   Maria called the office.

5. The movie started.   Ed arrived at the theater.

6. Ed fell asleep.   The movie ended.

7. Mr. Moto learned to speak English.   He came to the United States.

8. The train left.   Gloria got to the station.

PRACTICE 1 • *Combine the sentences using the past perfect with* **because.**

> He left his briefcase at home. He was upset.
> **He was upset because he'd left his briefcase at home.**
>
> She lost her key. She couldn't open the door.
> **She couldn't open the door because she'd lost her key.**

1. He worked very hard. He was tired.
2. She forgot to send the letter. He was angry with her.
3. I finished my work. I could relax.
4. We spent all our money. We couldn't go to the movies.
5. She studied economics. She knew something about money.
6. He sold his car. He couldn't drive to work.
7. He hurt his leg. He couldn't walk very fast.
8. She missed the party. She was disappointed.
9. She lost eighty pounds. I didn't recognize her.

WRITTEN EXERCISE • *Complete the sentences using* **so, because, if, unless,** *and* **although.**

> Your apartment will look better ____*if*____ you get some new furniture.
> I can't buy anything __*unless*__ I get a loan from the bank.

1. They're tired _____ they've worked all day without a break.
2. They won't work overtime _____ they get paid for it.
3. They don't like the manager, _____ they won't listen to him.
4. He took time to help me _____ he was in a hurry.
5. I don't go out much _____ I have very little free time.
6. You should get more exercise _____ you want to stay healthy.
7. We don't have a car, _____ we take the bus to work.
8. We're going to be late _____ we leave now.
9. I don't know _____ Mary is going to the meeting or not.
10. She's a nice person _____ she talks too much.

PRACTICE 2 • *Make questions about the sentences below.*

> Sam is looking at some hats.   He likes the gray one best.   It costs twenty dollars.
> **What is he looking at?**   **Which one does he like best?**   **How much does it cost?**

1. The boys have gone to the lake.
2. They left an hour ago.
3. They went by bus.
4. It takes three hours to get there.
5. They'll arrive at noon.
6. They plan to do some fishing.
7. The weather is very good.
8. There are five boats on the lake.
9. The red boat belongs to Doc Wiley.
10. He paid a thousand dollars for it.
11. Doc has been fishing since eight o'clock.
12. He's happy because the fishing is good.

People have many different kinds of problems as they go through life: medical, financial, occupational, or legal, and often these problems are related. For example, Anne's problem is both personal and occupational. She is dissatisfied with her work because it gives her very little opportunity for self-expression. Her dissatisfaction is so great that it affects her personal life, making her nervous and unhappy. In smaller towns like Wickam City, people who are having problems usually go to their friends or family for advice. They can also rely on the church for guidance and support.

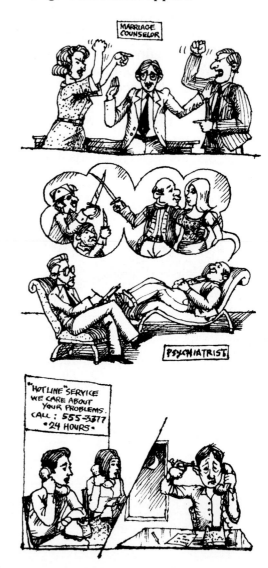

In larger urban areas, people often go to professional counselors for help in dealing with personal problems. Many cities in the United States provide family and marital counseling services to help resolve conflicts between members of the same family.

People who can afford it may go to a private psychiatrist for help. Psychiatrists often analyze their patient's dreams in order to gain a better understanding of their problems. Analysis can be very expensive, however, and for this reason many psychiatrists donate their time to public mental health clinics where people can receive counseling for a minimal fee. In Wickam City, Dr. Pasto gives free advice to just about anyone who comes to his door.

With the pressures of modern urban life, the lack of close personal relationships, and the increase in loneliness, suicide has become a serious concern. To try to prevent suicide, "hot lines" have been set up offering immediate help and advice to people in need. There are other "hot line" services covering a wide range of problems such as alcohol and drug addiction, wife beating, child abuse, and unwanted pregnancy.

As we have already seen in the case of Anne Jones, occupational difficulties may well cause serious personal as well as financial problems. People who are unemployed or in the wrong line of work might find the solution to their problems by going to an occupational counselor. Organizations and institutions offering help have increased enormously in recent years. There are so many of them nowadays that it can even be a problem finding the best place to get help for one's problems.

1. What are the major categories of problems for which people need help?
2. In smaller towns, where do people go for advice?
3. What is the purpose of family and marital counseling services?
4. Why do psychiatrists analyze their patients' dreams?
5. What are some of the causes of suicide?
6. How do "hot lines" try to prevent suicide?
7. What are some other problems covered by "hot line" services?

FREE RESPONSE

1. Who do you talk to when you need help with a personal problem?
2. When was the last time you got some good advice? How did it help you?
3. When was the last time you gave someone advice? Did it help or not?
4. Has anyone ever given you bad advice?
5. Do you read advice columns in newspapers or magazines?
6. What are some of the organizations offering help in your community?
7. Have you ever done volunteer work in your community? If so, what did you do?
8. Do you think we should help those who are close to us before we help others? In other words, do you think charity begins at home?

CLASS ACTIVITY • *Look at the pictures of Alice and Richard. What problems are they having in their marriage? What can they do to improve their relationship?*

ROLE PLAY

Student A plays a marriage counselor. Students B and C play a married couple.

Situation: The wife tells the marriage counselor about the problems she is having with her husband. Then the husband gives his side of the story. The marriage counselor listens to their problems, asks each of them some questions, and then tries to give them some good advice.

COMPOSITION

1. Write about an organization in your community that offers help to people in need.
2. Write about a time when you helped someone or someone helped you. Was the person a stranger or a friend?
3. Do you agree with those who say that charity begins at home? Why or why not?

VOCABULARY

actually
against
annoy
appointment
arm (n.)
arrange
awkward

brave (adj.)
bump (v.)

circumstances
convince
courage

dentist
desperate
difficulty
disaster
dissatisfied (adj.)
drop (n.)
dry (v.)

foolish
frustrated

hire (v.)

ice (n.)
into

kiss (n.)

lead (v.)
limited (adj.)
lousy

memory

naturally
nonsense

porch

ridiculous
risk (n.)
routine
ruin (v.)

shoulder (n.)
symptom

uninteresting (adj.)
until (conj.)
urgent
useless

water (v.)
whole

EXPRESSIONS

Hah!
What a life!
What a terrible morning!
You wouldn't believe it.

She was about to kiss Dr. Pasto.
She was accident prone.
She burst into tears.
It's such a struggle.

You poor dear.
We all have our bad moments.
I've got to run now.
This will only take a minute.

If I've told you once, I've told you a thousand times . . .
Nothing in life that is really worthwhile comes easily.

to be hard on someone
to go against one's nature
to make a mess of something
to run away from home

to fall apart
to fall asleep
to get upset
from now on

never mind
as soon as
on purpose
instead of

bad news
for instance
a rough draft
a great deal

PAST PERFECT: Affirmative

After	I'd (I had)	gotten dressed,	I left the house.
As soon as	she'd (she had)	eaten breakfast,	she went to work.
When	they'd (they had)	finished their coffee,	they called a taxi.

Interrogative

Had	you he they	been to the museum met Miss Hackey visited Los Angeles	before?

Short Answers

Yes,	you he they	had.

No,	you he they	hadn't.

WISH/IF ONLY

I wish If only	you	hadn't left. had waited for me.

HAVE/GET SOMETHING DONE

Barbara	had got	her eyes examined. the TV repaired.

She	had Dr. Squint examine got Tino to repair	her eyes. the TV.

VERB + OBJECT + INFINITIVE (without TO) MAKE

They	made	him her us	wash the dishes. clean the kitchen. take out the trash.

LET

He	let	her them me	use the computer. borrow his camera. see his photographs.

Chapter

Listen and repeat.

1

Gloria said (that) she was going to mail some letters.

2

Carlos said (that) he could play the trumpet.

3

Marty said (that) he didn't have any money.

4

Jenny said (that) she had lost her umbrella.

5

Tino told Barbara (that) he would wash the dishes.

6

Mabel told Sam (that) she hadn't made dinner.

PRACTICE 1 • *Change the sentences using reported speech.*

> Tino said, "I'm going to play tennis."
> **Tino said (that) he was going to play tennis.**
>
> Barbara said, "I haven't done the shopping yet."
> **Barbara said (that) she hadn't done the shopping yet.**

1. Maria said, "I want to buy a new hat."
2. Peter said, "I can't find my wallet."
3. Jenny said, "There's a good movie at the Odeon Theater."
4. Marty said, "I don't have any money."
5. Mr. Bascomb said, "I have a headache."
6. Mrs. Bascomb said, "I'll get some aspirin at the drugstore."
7. Dr. Pasto said, "It's going to rain."
8. Linda said, "I've finished cleaning the kitchen."
9. Jimmy said, "There isn't any food in the refrigerator."
10. Mabel said, "I didn't have time to go to the market."
11. Barney said, "I saw Nancy at the hospital."
12. Nancy said, "I'm feeling much better."

PRACTICE 2 • *Change the sentences using reported speech.*

> Tino said to Barbara, "I'll wash the dishes."
> **Tino told Barbara (that) he would wash the dishes.**
>
> Anne said to Mr. Bascomb, "You don't appreciate me."
> **Anne told Mr. Bascomb (that) he didn't appreciate her.**

1. Anne said to Dr. Pasto, "I don't like my job."
2. Dr. Pasto said to Anne, "You have to make a decision."
3. Mrs. Bascomb said to her husband, "You'll win the election."
4. Otis said to Gloria, "I won't let anyone build a toy factory in City Park."
5. Linda said to Jimmy, "Albert can take us to the beach in his car."
6. Sam said to Mabel, "I'm hungry."
7. Mabel said to Sam, "I didn't prepare anything for dinner."
8. Barney said to Nick, "My car needs a paint job."
9. Mona said to Fred, "I'm going to fix up the apartment."
10. Fred said to Mona, "I can't help you because I'm too busy."
11. Jenny said to Marty, "I've lost my umbrella."
12. Marty said to Jenny, "You left it at school."

FREE RESPONSE 1 • *Can you remember some things people have told you recently?*

> **My girlfriend told me (that) she didn't like my new shirt.**
> **My neighbor told me (that) he was going to quit his job.**

FREE RESPONSE 2 • *What are some things that you have told others?*

> **I told my mother (that) she made the best chocolate cake.**
> **I told the doctor (that) I'd never been in the hospital before.**

Listen and repeat.

Mrs. Golo told Marty to close the window.

She told him not to talk in class.

Dr. Molar told Gladys to open her mouth wide.

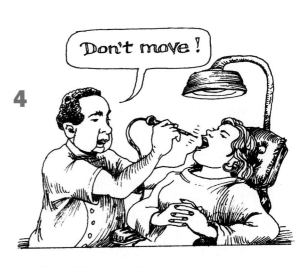

He told her not to move.

Blossom told Ed not to eat with his fingers.

She told him to use a knife and fork.

PRACTICE I • *Change the sentences using reported speech.*

> Maria said to Peter, "Write down your telephone number."
> **Maria told Peter to write down his telephone number.**
>
> Peter said to Maria, "Call me at the office."
> **Peter told Maria to call him at the office.**

1. Mabel said to Jimmy, "Feed the dog."
2. Sam said to Linda, "Finish your homework."
3. Mona said to Fred, "Get a job."
4. Dr. Pasto said to Anne, "Talk to Mr. Bascomb."
5. Tino said to Barbara, "Answer the telephone."
6. Mrs. Golo said to Marty, "Close the window."
7. Marty said to Jenny, "Meet me at the park."
8. Jenny said to Marty, "Bring some money."
9. Mona said to Fred, "Work hard."
10. Barney said to Fred, "Take it easy."
11. Linda said to Albert, "Wait for me."
12. Albert said to Linda, "Hurry up."

PRACTICE 2 • *Change the sentences using reported speech.*

> Mrs. Golo said to Jenny, "Don't talk to Marty."
> **Mrs. Golo told Jenny not to talk to Marty.**
>
> Marty said to Jenny, "Don't listen to Mrs. Golo."
> **Marty told Jenny not to listen to Mrs. Golo.**

1. Fred said to Marty, "Don't play in the street."
2. Marty said to Fred, "Don't worry."
3. Jimmy said to Linda, "Don't take so much time on the telephone."
4. Linda said to Jimmy, "Don't be in such a hurry."
5. Mr. Bascomb said to Anne, "Don't use the electric typewriter!"
6. Anne said to Mr. Bascomb, "Don't shout at me."
7. Mabel said to Sam, "Don't smoke your pipe in the living room!"
8. Sam said to Mabel, "Don't get excited."
9. Mona said to Fred, "Don't stay at the park too long."
10. Fred said to Mona, "Don't wait for me."
11. Mrs. Bascomb said to her husband, "Don't get mad at Anne."
12. Mr. Bascomb said to his wife, "Don't ask the impossible."

FREE RESPONSE I • *What have people told you to do recently?*

> **My mother told me not to talk to strangers.**
> **The teacher told me to pay attention in class.**

FREE RESPONSE 2 • *What have you told others to do?*

> **I told my roommate to clean up the apartment.**
> **I told the barber not to cut my hair too short.**

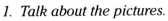
1. Talk about the pictures.
2. Listen to the story.
3. Answer the story questions.

Yesterday morning Johnnie was working at the bookshop when he heard a loud noise. He looked out the window and saw something that horrified him. A large bus had just crashed into a truck. The driver of the bus had tried to avoid hitting a boy riding his bicycle in the street. He had turned sharply and crashed into a truck parked on the side of the street.

Johnnie saw at least ten people getting out of the bus and heard them calling for help. He ran across the street to give assistance. Suddenly he felt someone grab his arm. It was an old lady who had been in the bus. She had lost her handbag and was terribly upset. Johnnie looked for the handbag and found it lying near the bus. He was about to return it to the lady when a police officer came up behind him. The officer asked Johnnie if there was a telephone in the bookshop. Johnnie told him there was a telephone by the cash register. The officer ran over to the bookshop and called an ambulance.

Johnnie felt smoke getting in his eyes and took off his glasses. A few minutes later an ambulance came and took some people to the hospital for X-rays. A couple of people were slightly injured in the accident, but no one was seriously hurt. Suzi Suzuki, a reporter for a local TV news station, came and interviewed a few people at the scene of the accident. Johnnie Wilson was among them.

1. What did Johnnie hear yesterday as he was working at the bookshop?
2. What had just happened?
3. How many people did Johnnie see getting out of the bus?
4. Were they calling for help?
5. Who grabbed Johnnie's arm?
6. Why was she upset?
7. Where did Johnnie find the handbag?
8. What did the police officer ask Johnnie?
9. Did the police officer use the phone to call his girlfriend?
10. Who is Suzi Suzuki and what did she do?

PRACTICE • *Combine the sentences as indicated.*

Johnnie saw the passengers. They were getting out of the bus.
Johnnie saw the passengers getting out of the bus.

He heard them. They were calling for help.
He heard them calling for help.

1. Johnnie found the old lady's handbag. It was lying near the bus.
2. We heard Johnnie. He was talking about the accident.
3. I smelled smoke. It was coming from the bus.
4. Dr. Pasto caught Marty. He was taking some apples.
5. Albert saw Linda. She was standing by the bus stop.
6. We heard children. They were singing in the church.
7. I felt the rain. It was falling on my head.
8. Peter watched the boys. They were playing football.
9. Jimmy found the dog. It was sleeping on the couch.

Listen and practice.

SUZI: I'm Suzi Suzuki reporting on a major traffic accident. Standing next to me is a man who can tell us all about it. What is your name and occupation, sir?

JOHNNIE: My name is Johnnie Wilson. I'm the owner of Johnnie's Bookshop.

SUZI: Where were you when the accident took place, Mr. Wilson?

JOHNNIE: I was in the bookshop.

SUZI: Did you see the bus crash into the truck?

JOHNNIE: No, but I heard it. It made a very loud noise.

SUZI: Do you know what caused the accident?

JOHNNIE: I heard someone say there was a boy riding his bicycle in the street. The bus driver tried to avoid hitting him. He made a sudden turn and lost control of the bus.

SUZI: What did you do after the bus crashed into the truck?

JOHNNIE: I came running over to help.

SUZI: Were you the one who called the ambulance?

JOHNNIE: No, a police officer called the ambulance. He used the telephone in my shop.

SUZI: Is there anything else you would like to add, Mr. Wilson?

JOHNNIE: Yes, my bookshop is located at the corner of Lime Street and Third Avenue. We're open daily from . . .

SUZI: Thank you, Mr. Wilson. This has been a live interview at the scene of the accident. I'm Suzi Suzuki reporting for KWIC News. Good afternoon.

WRITTEN EXERCISE • *An hour later, an investigator came and asked Johnnie some questions about the accident. Complete the conversation between Johnnie and the investigator. Compare with a partner.*

INVESTIGATOR: Mr. Wilson, I want you to be as accurate as possible. Tell me only what you *saw* with your own eyes and *heard* with your own ears.

JOHNNIE: Yes, sir.

INVESTIGATOR: Did you *see* the bus crash into the truck?

JOHNNIE: No. I heard it *crash into the truck*. I was in the bookstore across the street.

INVESTIGATOR: What happened then?

JOHNNIE: I saw the _____ get out of the bus.

INVESTIGATOR: Did they call for help?

JOHNNIE: Yes. I heard them _____.

INVESTIGATOR: What about the old lady? Did she say something to you?

JOHNNIE: Yes. She _____ me that she had lost her handbag. _____ very upset.

INVESTIGATOR: What happened? Did you find her handbag?

JOHNNIE: Yes. It was near the bus. A police officer _____ me pick it up and give it _____.

INVESTIGATOR: A police officer? Was he the one who called the ambulance?

JOHNNIE: Yes, he was. My assistant heard him _____. They got here right away.

INVESTIGATOR: How many people did they take to the hospital?

JOHNNIE: I _____ them _____ three people. I hope they're all right.

INVESTIGATOR: I hope so, too. Thank you for your help.

Ever since Anne became a secretary at the City Bank, Mr. Bascomb had been dissatisfied with her work. She had trouble counting money, she couldn't type very well, and she was always forgetting things. Anne often appeared to be dreaming, as if her mind were on something else besides her work. In fact, she did spend a lot of time thinking about her music and often imagined herself singing before an enthusiastic audience.

Mr. Bascomb thought that he had been fair to Anne. He had given her plenty of time to improve her work. And he had warned her repeatedly that if she didn't start doing better she would be out of a job. He hoped that eventually Anne would take her work seriously and become a good secretary, but she never did. After discussing the situation with his wife, Mr. Bascomb finally decided to fire Anne. Yesterday he called her into his office to give her the news.

"Anne, come into my office, please. I want to talk to you."
"Yes, Mr. Bascomb. What is it?"
"I'm not happy with your work, Anne. You've been making even more mistakes than usual. It's obvious that you aren't suited for this kind of job. I'm afraid . . ."
"I have a few complaints, too, Mr. Bascomb," interrupted Anne.
"Oh really? What seems to be the problem?"

"You take advantage of me. A secretary shouldn't have to do personal errands for her boss."

"What are you talking about?" said Mr. Bascomb. A cold, hard expression came over his face.

Anne was very uncomfortable, but she was determined to take a stand. "I'm talking about all the times you've asked me to buy presents for your wife. And all the times I've had to make coffee and get sandwiches for you. Not to mention all the times I've had to come here on the weekend and clean up your office."

"What's wrong with that?" asked Mr. Bascomb. "You don't have anything better to do with your time."

"That's what you think. The truth is, I've been wasting my time working at City Bank. I have much better things to do. I'm going to be a professional singer."

Mr. Bascomb started laughing. "You're funny, Anne. You can't even type a simple business letter. What makes you think you have the talent to be a professional singer?"

Anne looked Mr. Bascomb straight in the eye. "You think because you're a big banker that you know everything. What makes you think you have the brains to be mayor of Wickam City?"

Mr. Bascomb's mouth dropped open. He could hardly believe his ears. "I knew I'd made a mistake when I hired you," he said. "You're nothing but a dumb female who doesn't know her place."

"I'm not dumb enough to vote for you. That's for sure."

Mr. Bascomb was furious. He could hardly control himself. "You're fired!" he said, pointing to the door. "Get out!"

"That's fine with me," said Anne. "I never liked this job anyway."

Barbara saw Anne run out of Mr. Bascomb's office and went over to her.

"I heard you arguing with Mr. Bascomb," she said. "What happened?"

Anne hesitated for a minute to catch her breath. "He said he wasn't happy with my work."

"Then what happened?"

"I told him I had a few complaints of my own. I said that a secretary shouldn't have to do personal errands for her boss."

"You were right, Anne. What else did you say?"

"I told him that I'd been wasting my time working at City Bank and that I had better things to do."

"What was Mr. Bascomb's reaction?"

"He called me a dumb female and said I couldn't even type a simple business letter."

"That wasn't very nice. What happened then?"

"I told Mr. Bascomb that I wasn't dumb enough to vote for him. Then he got mad and fired me. He pointed to the door and told me to get out."

"Did you say anything before you left?"

"Yes, I told him that I never liked being a secretary anyway."

"Oh, Anne, I'm so proud of you. It took real courage to stand up to Mr. Bascomb. But what are you going to do now?"

"I'm going to pack my bags and go to Hollywood. I'm going to be a professional singer."

"That's fantastic," said Barbara. "I hope you make it. Good luck, Anne."

STORY QUESTIONS

1. Why did Mr. Bascomb call Anne into his office?
2. What did Anne complain about?
3. What did Mr. Bascomb do about Anne's complaints?
4. How did he react when Anne said she was going to be a professional singer?
5. What did Anne and Mr. Bascomb say to each other that was unkind?
6. How did their conversation end?
7. Why was Barbara proud of Anne?
8. Do you think Anne made a mistake by complaining to Mr. Bascomb? Why?
9. Do you think Mr. Bascomb was right to fire Anne? Why?

ROLE PLAY • *Student A plays Anne and Student B plays Mr. Bascomb. Act out the conversation between Anne and Mr. Bascomb with your books closed.*

PAIR WORK • *Franco Fellini is directing Ula Hackey in a new movie. Can you think of more things he might tell her to do in this scene? Make a list of at least four commands and read them to the class.*

LISTENING • *First, listen to the directions that are given to Miss Hackey by the director. Then try to remember what he told her to do.*

First, he told her to go to the table.

Mabel said to Sam, "My sister called yesterday. She's going to be in Wickam City this week."

Mabel told Sam that her sister had called the day before. She was going to be in Wickam City that week.

Sam said to Mabel, "We'll have to clean up the house tomorrow. It looks terrible."

Sam told Mabel that they would have to clean up the house the next day. It looked terrible.

1. Mr. Bascomb said to Anne, "I'm not happy with your work."

_____

2. Anne said to Mr. Bascomb, "I have a few complaints, too."

_____

3. Nancy said to Barney, "Vote for Otis."

_____

4. Barney said to Nancy, "I'll make up my own mind."

_____

5. Anne said to Mr. Bascomb, "I'm going to be a professional singer."

_____

6. Mr. Bascomb said to Anne, "You can't even type a simple business letter."

_____

7. Nancy said to Barney, "I've never been in love."

_____

8. Barney said to Nancy, "Don't worry. Some day you'll meet the right man."

_____

9. Barbara said to Tino, "You look tired."

_____

10. Tino said to Barbara, "I didn't sleep very well last night."

_____

11. Mr. Bascomb said to his wife, "Everything went wrong this morning."

_____

12. Mrs. Bascomb said to her husband, "You'll feel better when you've had something to eat."

_____

WRITTEN EXERCISE • *Complete the sentences about the pictures. Describe what each person saw, felt, or heard using the gerund form of these verbs:* **argue, blow, cry, dance, fall, get, play, ride, swim.**

1. Barbara *heard* Anne *arguing* with Mr. Bascomb.

2. Johnnie *felt* smoke *getting* in his eyes.

3. Jenny *saw* a clown *riding* a bicycle.

4. Maria _____ the wind _____ her hair.

5. Fred _____ a baby _____ in the theater.

6. Barney _____ Ula Hackey _____ with Antonio.

7. Gloria _____ someone _____ the violin.

8. Mrs. Golo _____ a dog _____ in the pond.

9. Mr. Bascomb _____ raindrops _____ on his head.

FREE RESPONSE • *Describe something you saw, felt, or heard earlier today or yesterday.*

Since the early 1960s, there have been many changes in American society as a direct result of the women's movement. Feminists are telling women they don't have to conform to expected social roles that limit their freedom. The feminists believe that women should be able to act from a position of choice, so they can do what they want in life. Nowadays women are turning to many jobs that used to be for men only; they are becoming mechanics, politicians, and even soldiers.

In spite of the considerable gains that women have made, many feminists argue that women still have a long way to go. They point out that women often receive lower pay than men for doing the same work and, in many cases, men still get preference in hiring and promotions. There are some male employers, like Mr. Bascomb, who take advantage of their female employees by making them do personal errands. This kind of job discrimination makes women feel like "second-class citizens."

Some feminist groups think that women will achieve equality only through basic changes in society. These groups say men should help with the housework and child care to free women for outside work. They believe this would result in relationships between men and women based on mutual interests, respect, and affection, rather than on men's economic and physical dominance.

The women's movement encourages women to be more assertive and to express their feelings openly. Women are being told they don't have to accept a passive role in society or in their relationships with men. This is causing confusion among many people who don't know what is expected of them and are unsure about how to react to new and different situations. With women becoming more aggressive, the following scene is no longer unthinkable: A woman calls up a man she knows and invites him out for the evening. She picks him up, insists on paying for the tickets to the movie, and also pays the bill in the restaurant. Now, how does this man feel? At first he might feel flattered by all the attention he is getting, only to start feeling confused and embarrassed as the evening progresses. Or he might enjoy the whole thing from beginning to end. It depends on the man.

This is just one small example of how things have changed. Similar occurrences are also taking place in the world of business, politics, and sports. Although a large number of American women support the women's movement, there are many others who oppose its objectives. These women see the women's movement as a threat to the family and traditional values. They point out that it's very difficult for women to have full-time careers and be good mothers. So there is a lot of disagreement about women's rights. But regardless of one's viewpoint, one cannot deny that the women's movement, in raising issues that affect women, is having an impact on people's lives in America and all over the world.

1. What is the message of the women's movement? What are the feminists saying?
2. What are some traditional "male" professions that women are now entering?
3. In what ways are women still being discriminated against?
4. What are some of the changes that feminist groups are seeking?
5. How will male-female relationships change if the feminists are successful?
6. Do you think women should be more or less assertive than they are now? Why?
7. Do you think it's okay for a woman to ask a man out for a date?
8. Why do some women oppose the women's movement?

FREE RESPONSE

1. Do you think women should be allowed to do any job? Why or why not?
2. Name some jobs that are thought to be typically "male" or "female."
3. Do you think women with young children should have full-time careers?
4. How do men in your country feel about their wives working outside the home?
5. Do you believe that a woman's place is in the home?
6. Do women in your country have the same problems as women in the United States?
7. How strong is the women's movement in your country?
8. Do you think some changes are necessary?

GROUP DISCUSSION • *How do you feel about the women's movement? Do you think it's good for everyone? Why or why not? Give reasons for your opinions.*

GROUP WORK • *How are men and women different? Make a list of five basic differences and share your findings with the class.*

COMPOSITION

1. Write about the women's movement. Do you agree with its objectives? Why or why not?
2. Describe your ideal man or woman. What qualities does he or she have? How is he or she different from other men or women?

add	dumb	horrify	smoke (n.)
ambulance			sudden
among	enthusiastic	mention (v.)	
assistance	eventually		terribly
assistant (n.)		occupation	turn (n.)
	female		
brain (n.)	feminist	reaction	warn
	furious	repeatedly	
control (n.)			
control (v.)	grab	slightly	

EXPRESSIONS

ever since	to be located	to know one's place
more than usual	to take place	to stand up to someone
at the scene	to do an errand	to take something seriously

She was determined to take a stand.
She looked him straight in the eye.
You take advantage of me.
I've been wasting my time.

What seems to be the problem?
What's wrong with that?
That wasn't very nice.
That's for sure.

You're fired!
That's fine with me.
He could hardly believe his ears.
That's what you think.

I'm so proud of you.
That's fantastic!
I hope you make it.
Good luck.

DIRECT SPEECH

General Statements	REPORTED SPEECH (SAY)
She said, "They're leaving today." He said, "Anne called yesterday." They said, "We can't work tomorrow."	She said (that) they were leaving that day. He said (that) Anne had called the day before. They said (that) they couldn't work the next day.

DIRECT SPEECH

Statements to a Particular Person	REPORTED SPEECH (TELL)
She said to Nick, "I like my job." I said to Jimmy, "I've met your father." Bob said to Jane, "I won't forget you."	She told Nick (that) she liked her job. I told Jimmy (that) I had met his father. Bob told Jane (that) he wouldn't forget her.

MODALS

Mona said to Fred, "You should buy a car." Fred said to Mona, "I would if I could."	Mona told Fred (that) he should buy a car. Fred told Mona (that) he would if he could.
I said to her, "I might not be on time." She said to me, "You could if you tried."	I told her (that) I might not be on time. She told me (that) I could if I tried.

IMPERATIVE

He said to Linda, "Open the window." I said to Marty, "Call Mrs. Golo."	He told Linda to open the window. I told Marty to call Mrs. Golo.
She said, "Don't walk on the grass." They said, "Don't wait for us."	She said not to walk on the grass. They said not to wait for them.

VERB + OBJECT + INFINITIVE (without TO) or GERUND

She	heard	him	play (playing) the piano.
He	felt	her	touch (touching) his arm.
We	saw	them	leave (leaving) the house.

Chapter 3

Listen and repeat.

Marty asked Jenny if she liked westerns.

Jenny asked her mother if she was going to make a cake.

Fred asked Barney if he had seen Marty.

Fred asked Marty if he had gotten into a fight.

Gloria asked Dr. Pasto if he could play jazz.

Tino asked Barbara if she would be ready soon.

PRACTICE • *Suzi Suzuki is interviewing Mr. Bascomb about his campaign for mayor. Change her questions to reported speech.*

> "Are you in a hurry, Mr. Bascomb?" asked Suzi.
> **She asked him if he was in a hurry.**
>
> "Can you give me a few minutes of your time?"
> **She asked him if he could give her a few minutes of his time.**

1. "Are you satisfied with your campaign so far?"
2. "Do you expect to win the election?"
3. "Did you hear Otis's last speech?"
4. "Are you going to debate Otis?"
5. "Do you plan to appear on television?"
6. "Have you spent a lot of money on your campaign?"
7. "Did you fire your secretary?"
8. "Does your wife help you?"
9. "Can you improve city government?"
10. "Can you bring more business to Wickam City?"
11. "Will you lower taxes?"
12. "Will you provide more jobs?"

FREE RESPONSE 1 • *Can you remember some things people have asked you recently?*

> **My neighbor asked me if I wanted to sell my car.**
> **Mary asked me if I had taken her dictionary.**

FREE RESPONSE 2 • *What have you asked others?*

> **I asked Miss Romantica if I could have her phone number.**
> **I asked my brother if he knew a good place to go dancing.**

Listen and repeat.

1

Marty asked Jenny what she was reading.

Nick asked Barney where he could get a good haircut.

3

Linda asked Sam why he always wore the same hat.

Barbara asked Anne when she (had) started playing the guitar.

5

Fred asked Blossom how long she had been waiting for the bus.

Luisa asked Carlos when he would be back.

PRACTICE • *Johnnie ran into Anne yesterday on the way home. He hadn't seen her for a long time and had a lot of questions to ask her. Change his questions to reported speech.*

> "How are you, Anne?" asked Johnnie.
> **He asked her how she was.**
>
> "When did we last see each other?"
> **He asked her when they had last seen each other.**

1. "Where have you been?"
2. "Why did you quit your job?"
3. "What are you going to do?"
4. "Why do you want to be a singer?"
5. "When did you make up your mind?"
6. "How can you leave Wickam City?"
7. "When will you go to Hollywood?"
8. "How much money do you have?"
9. "Where will you stay?"
10. "How will you get an audition?"
11. "Who's going to help you?"
12. "When will I see you again?"

FREE RESPONSE 1 • *Report a question that someone has asked you recently using one of these words: **what, when, where, why, who, how.***

> **My boyfriend asked me where I learned to dance.**
> **Ms. Drake asked me when I was going home.**

FREE RESPONSE 2 • *Report a question you have asked someone recently.*

> **I asked my sister why she hadn't gone to the market.**
> **I asked Robert how he could tell the time without a watch.**

1. *Talk about the picture.*
2. *Listen to the story.*
3. *Answer the story questions.*

There has been a lot of excitement in Wickam City recently because of the election campaign for mayor. Last week a debate was held between the two candidates, Otis Jackson and John Bascomb. Debates are not usually held before elections in Wickam City, but this year a special request was made by the City Council. They wanted the people to know exactly who and what they were voting for. The debate was held in the Civic Auditorium, where 1,000 people can be seated. Tickets were not sold for the debate; it was free for anyone who wanted to go. As expected, a large number of people came to hear Otis and Mr. Bascomb. The debate was scheduled to begin at seven o'clock but was delayed fifteen minutes so that everyone could be seated.

The two candidates were introduced by Dr. Pasto, even though everyone in town already knew them. Questions were presented by a group of reporters and the candidates were given a couple of minutes to prepare their thoughts. Mr. Bascomb, whose banking position has given him a lot of experience in dealing with the public, was a very good speaker. He presented his ideas for improving Wickam City. He wanted a toy factory to be built in City Park in order to bring more jobs and money to the city. This was a very controversial issue, and many people in the audience disagreed with Mr. Bascomb. He was interrupted several times when it was his turn to speak.

Otis, whose formal speaking experience is fairly limited, spoke in a conversational manner. He felt that City Park should be kept for the people to enjoy. Various other topics such as public transportation and education were also debated. The opinions given on these subjects were also quite different. By the time the debate ended at nine o'clock, the whole auditorium was alive with discussion. Naturally, the debate was not attended by everyone in town, and for those who did not go, it was broadcast on the local radio station. Coffee was served after the debate, and this gave people a better chance to talk with Otis and Mr. Bascomb.

1. Why did the City Council want Otis and Mr. Bascomb to have a debate?
2. Where was the debate held?
3. When was the debate scheduled to begin?
4. Who introduced the candidates?
5. Why did Mr. Bascomb want a toy factory to be built in City Park?
6. Why was he interrupted when it was his turn to speak?
7. Why didn't Otis want a toy factory to be built in City Park?
8. What other topics were debated?

PRACTICE • *Change the sentences using the passive voice.*

The City Council held a debate last week.	They served coffee after the debate.
A debate was held last week.	**Coffee was served after the debate.**

1. The organizers held the debate in the Civic Auditorium.
2. They scheduled the debate to begin at seven o'clock.
3. They delayed the debate for fifteen minutes.
4. Dr. Pasto introduced the candidates.
5. The reporters asked questions.
6. They gave the candidates three minutes to answer the questions.
7. The audience interrupted Mr. Bascomb several times.
8. The organizers broadcast the debate on the radio.
9. They interviewed both candidates after the debate.

Listen and practice.

After the debate Peter and Maria got into an argument. Maria thought Otis was right, while Peter defended Mr. Bascomb's position.

MARIA: You know, I think Otis is right about City Park. It should be kept for the people to enjoy.

PETER: A lot of people agree with Otis on that point. But, in my opinion, Mr. Bascomb is the best candidate for mayor.

MARIA: Why, Peter?

PETER: Because he's promised to lower taxes and provide more jobs.

MARIA: Do you really think he'll keep his promises?

PETER: Yes, Mr. Bascomb is a man of his word. We can count on him.

MARIA: I think we'd be better off with Otis. The things he says make a lot of sense to me.

PETER: I know you support Otis. And I like him personally. But he doesn't have the knowledge or experience to be mayor.

MARIA: He should be given a chance, Peter. He can't be expected to know everything.

PETER: He doesn't have to know everything, but he should have definite plans for improving the city.

MARIA: Like Mr. Bascomb?

PETER: Yes. Mr. Bascomb has a lot of good ideas, and he's a leader. He knows how to organize and get things done.

MARIA: Otis is also a leader. He has a rare ability to inspire people. I think a lot will be accomplished if he's elected.

PETER: Well, it'll be interesting to see what happens.

WRITTEN EXERCISE • *Change the sentences using the passive voice.*

The voters will choose a new mayor next month.

A new mayor will be chosen next month.

Most people expect Mr. Bascomb to win.

Mr. Bascomb is expected to win.

Reporters have interviewed him on television and radio.

He has been interviewed on television and radio.

1. Someone told me that you're for Otis.

   _____

2. Most people respect him for being honest.

   _____

3. His supporters have raised thousands of dollars for his campaign.

   _____

4. They have planned a special dinner for Otis.

   _____

5. They are going to hold the event at the Wickam Hotel.

   _____

6. They have already sold two hundred tickets.

   _____

7. They will use the money to help Otis win the election.

   _____

PRACTICE • *Change the sentences using the passive voice.*

They should save City Park.   They should build a new hospital.
City Park should be saved.   **A new hospital should be built.**

1. They should lower taxes.
2. They should provide more jobs.
3. They should give more money to education.
4. They should build more schools.
5. They should repair the streets.
6. They should improve public transportation.
7. They should eliminate pollution.
8. They should do more to stop crime.

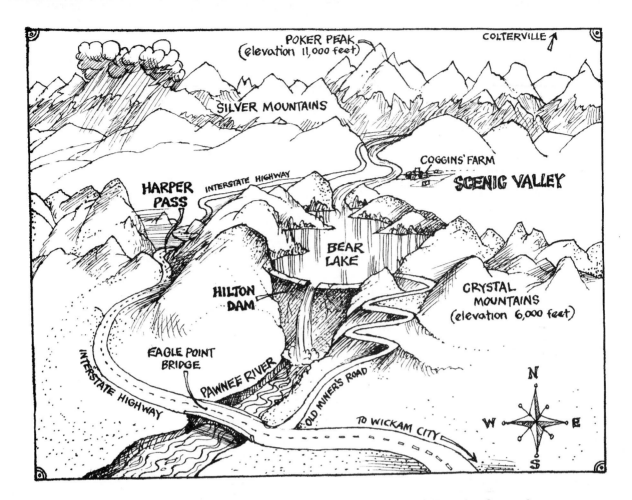

For several months there had been unusually heavy rainfall in the Crystal Mountains near Wickam City. The Pawnee River had risen several feet and Bear Lake had increased to almost twice its normal size. Many residents of Wickam City were afraid that Hilton Dam would not be able to hold so much water. The dam had been built before the Second World War and needed to be reinforced. However, nothing could be done until after the rains had stopped. As each day passed, the people in the area became more and more worried. Last Friday their greatest fear was realized: Hilton Dam burst, sending a great flood of water toward the sea.

Wickam City wasn't hit by the flood, but many farmers in the surrounding area were forced to leave their homes. Communication was maintained by radio since most telephone lines had been knocked down. Dozens of calls for help were received, including an urgent message from Sarah Coggins. Her husband, Elmer, was very sick and needed medicine right away. The Coggins's farm is located in Scenic Valley about twenty miles north of the Crystal Mountains. Since the dam burst it was impossible to send them supplies by land. The interstate highway couldn't be used because the bridge crossing the Pawnee River had been destroyed by the flood. City officials didn't expect to have it repaired before spring. A temporary bridge was being built, but it wouldn't be completed for at least a week. The Old Miner's Road was flooded and couldn't be used, either. And the interstate highway from Colterville to Scenic Valley was closed because of heavy snowfall in the Silver Mountains.

The only way to reach the Coggins's farm was by air. Yesterday a rescue mission was planned by the mayor of Wickam City. It was announced on the radio that Nancy Paine had been chosen to make the flight. She was the logical choice since she knew the area better than anyone else. By coincidence, Nancy had a special reason of her own for wanting to help the Coggins family. A few months earlier she had crashed into their barn and Elmer had driven her over fifty miles to the nearest hospital. Although she hadn't completely recovered from her accident, she felt that she had to make the flight.

Nancy was given a map and some medicine to take to Elmer. She was advised to fly around the Crystal Mountains as it was considered too dangerous to fly over them. A special plane was made ready for the flight. When Nancy got to the airport, the engine had already been serviced and the tank filled up with gas. A number of people were there to wish her luck. Nancy smiled and waved to her friends as she took off.

Nancy's rescue mission was a success. She delivered the medicine to Elmer Coggins and returned safely to Wickam City. When she arrived at the airport, a large crowd was there to receive her. They all wanted to shake her hand and congratulate her on a job well done. Nancy was very tired, but she shook hands with everyone. She was considered a real heroine.

STORY QUESTIONS

1. What caused the dam to burst?
2. How did the flood affect the farmers in the surrounding area?
3. How was communication maintained?
4. Why did Sarah Coggins send an urgent call for help?
5. Where is the Coggins's farm located?
6. Why was it impossible to send supplies to the Coggins's farm by land?
7. What was the only way to reach the Coggins's farm?
8. Who was chosen to fly the rescue mission?
9. What was Nancy's special reason for wanting to make the flight?
10. What did Nancy deliver to Elmer?
11. Why was Nancy considered a heroine?

TALKING ABOUT HEROES

1. Have you ever heard about someone who risked his or her life to come to the aid of another person?
2. Do you think there are more heroes in the movies or in real life?
3. Who are your heroes? Why are they your heroes?
4. Do you know of any cases when a person was in trouble and no one helped? Why do some people refuse to help others?
5. What would you do if you saw another person in trouble? Would you know what to do if someone was having a heart attack or choking on a piece of food?

PAIR WORK • *After Nancy had completed her mission, she was interviewed by Suzi Suzuki. Practice reading their conversation with a partner.*

(1) SUZI: Nancy, can I talk to you? I need an interview for the news.

(2) NANCY: Will it take long? I'm very tired.

(3) SUZI: It'll only take a few minutes. I don't have many questions.

(4) NANCY: Go ahead. I'm ready.

(5) SUZI: Why did they choose you to make the flight?

(6) NANCY: I know the area better than anyone else.

(7) SUZI: Did you have any problems during your flight?

(8) NANCY: There was a lot of wind and rain. But I'm used to flying in bad weather.

(9) SUZI: Where did you land? There's nothing but farmland in Scenic Valley.

(10) NANCY: I was forced to land in Elmer's wheatfield.

(11) SUZI: How is Elmer doing?

(12) NANCY: He's still sick, but he's going to be all right.

(13) SUZI: Do you plan to make any more flights?

(14) NANCY: I'll fly if they need me. But I hope it won't be necessary.

(15) SUZI: Wickam City is very proud of you, Nancy. You're a real heroine.

(16) NANCY: Thank you. But I'm not sure I deserve so much attention.

(17) SUZI: You're too modest. You made an extraordinary flight and saved a man's life.

(18) NANCY: It's part of my job.

(19) SUZI: What are you going to do when you get home?

(20) NANCY: I'm going to take a long rest.

(21) SUZI: You certainly deserve it. Thank you for the interview, Nancy.

(22) NANCY: Don't mention it. The public has a right to know.

PRACTICE • *Report what was said in the conversation.*

(1) Suzi asked Nancy if she could talk to her. She needed an interview for the news.
(2) Nancy asked if it would take long. She was very tired.
(3) Suzi said it would only take a few minutes. She didn't have many questions.

LISTENING • *In most conversations, there are key words we use to communicate the main points. Listen for the key words in the conversation between (1) Mr. Bascomb and Mrs. Warbucks.*

Key words:

money	haven't decided
campaign	plans for Wickam City
contribution	

CONVERSATION • *Gladys heard the conversation between Mr. Bascomb and Mrs. Warbucks. Now she's telling her friend, Rita, what she heard. Listen and practice.*

GLADYS: Guess what! I heard Mr. Bascomb talking with Mrs. Warbucks at the Country Club!

RITA: Oh, really? What did they talk about?

GLADYS: Money! Mr. Bascomb asked Mrs. Warbucks if she would make a contribution to his campaign.

RITA: What did she say?

GLADYS: She hadn't decided yet. She said she wanted to know more about his plans for Wickam City.

PAIR WORK • *Imagine you were at the Country Club and you heard the conversation between (2) Ula Hackey and Antonio. Your partner, who wasn't at the party, wants to know what the famous couple talked about. To make this exercise more challenging, your partner leaves the room while you listen to the recorded conversation. Write down the key words and tell your partner what you heard. Have a conversation similar to the conversation between Gladys and Rita.*

WRITTEN EXERCISE 1 • *Work in pairs. Write a dialogue of eight to twelve lines based on one of the conversations you heard on page 54. Try to make the conversation lively and interesting.*

Situation 1: Mr. Bascomb tries to convince Mrs. Warbucks to give money to his campaign. Mrs. Warbucks wants to know what Mr. Bascomb will do if he wins the election.

Situation 2: Antonio tries to convince Miss Hackey to marry him and go to Spain. Ula Hackey adores Antonio, but she doesn't want to give up her career.

ROLE PLAY • *Act out one of the above dialogues before the class without looking at the script.*

WRITTEN EXERCISE 2 • *Complete the sentences using the passive voice.*

My favorite movie, *Citizen Kane*, *will be shown* on TV next week.
(show)

It *is considered* one of the greatest movies ever made.
(consider)

Citizen Kane *was directed* by Orson Welles.
(direct)

1. Dr. Pasto's house _____ in 1892.
(build)

2. The gate _____ for a long time.
(break)

3. Dr. Pasto says the gate _____ tomorrow.
(repair)

4. Last Sunday the football game _____ because of rain.
(delay)

5. All of the home games _____ at Wickam Stadium.
(play)

6. Tickets for next Sunday's game _____ at the box office now.
(sell)

7. Several months ago a decision _____ to build a new highway.
(make)

8. So far, more than $500,000 _____ on the highway.
(spend)

9. The highway _____ by a five-cent tax on gasoline.
(finance)

10. The highway _____ next year.
(complete)

In a few weeks the people of Wickam City will elect their next mayor. It is important that they choose a good leader. What should the voters be thinking about as they make their decision? What qualities are important for a leader to have?

In our opinion, a leader should be able to organize and inspire. Some leaders, like Mr. Bascomb, are very good organizers while others, such as Otis, are very good at inspiring people. The most successful leaders are able to both organize and inspire. They know how to plan a campaign, delegate tasks, and get the cooperation of other people.

Leaders who have good organizing ability are very disciplined and make efficient use of their time. They work hard and pay attention to details. Their campaigns are carefully planned with an awareness of their opponents' strengths and weaknesses. They assign tasks to their followers and then make sure that these jobs are done. They choose the right person for the right job. They tell their people exactly what they are supposed to do and make them perform. They have good judgment. They give careful consideration to each problem before they take action. And they accept responsibility. They are willing to make difficult decisions and stand by those decisions.

To be an inspiring leader, a person must possess a number of outstanding personal qualities, including honesty, determination, and enthusiasm. Enthusiasm is probably the most important. As Ralph Waldo Emerson said, "Nothing great was ever achieved without enthusiasm." A leader who lacks energy will find it very hard to inspire others to work hard.

To be inspiring, leaders must be honest. They must speak the truth and their words must be supported by their actions. They cannot say one thing and do another. They cannot claim to have a true concern for those they represent while actually seeking personal gain. Such people will lose the trust and confidence of their followers. As Abraham Lincoln once said, "You can fool some of the people all of the time, and all of the people some of the time, but you can't fool all of the people all of the time."

Great leaders must inspire their followers to fight for what they believe in. They must have high standards of personal conduct and set an example by their actions. They must be determined; they cannot be discouraged by the problems they encounter. They must prepare to fight a long battle if necessary. And they must have faith. They must believe in the justice of their cause and in its ultimate victory.

1. What must a leader be able to do?
2. Why is Mr. Bascomb a good leader?
3. Why is Otis Jackson a good leader?
4. Describe a good organizer. What does he or she do?
5. What qualities must an inspirational leader have?
6. Why is enthusiasm so important?
7. How do leaders show that they are honest? What must they do?
8. What will happen to a dishonest leader?
9. What did Abraham Lincoln say about fooling the people?
10. How do leaders show their determination?
11. What does it mean for a leader to have faith?

FREE RESPONSE

1. What famous leader do you admire? Why do you look up to this person?
2. What are his or her outstanding qualities?
3. Do you think the current president of the United States is a great leader? Why or why not?
4. Do you think there are more great leaders today than in the past?
5. Do you think great leaders are born or made?
6. What qualities do you think are necessary for a leader to have?
7. Do you consider yourself a leader? Why or why not?
8. Do you see yourself becoming a leader at some point in the future?

GROUP WORK 1 • *Discuss great leaders in the history of your country. What did these leaders do that changed the lives of their fellow citizens?*

TALKING ABOUT DEBATES

Debates are very important in American elections. They often decide which candidates win. It is believed that Abraham Lincoln and John F. Kennedy were elected president of the United States because they performed well in their debates.

1. Who was Kennedy's opponent in the presidential debates of 1960?
2. Have you ever seen or heard a political debate? If so, who were the contestants? What issues were they debating?
3. What do you think is the most important factor in winning a debate: the person's looks, personality, intelligence, or speaking ability?
4. What difference does it make if people see a political debate on television or hear it on the radio?
5. If you were a campaign manager, what advice would you give your candidate before a television debate?

PAIR WORK • *Tell your partner about an interesting interview you heard on TV or radio recently. The interview could be with a political leader, an author, or any prominent individual. Answer your partner's questions about the interview. Find out if you both agree or disagree with the statements made by the person being interviewed.*

GROUP WORK 2 • *Make an invitation list for a dinner party. Choose the five most interesting people you can think of. Give reasons for your choices. The people on your list should all be famous or prominent individuals. Share your invitation list with the class.*

COMPOSITION

1. Write about a famous world leader or an important leader in your country. How has this person demonstrated leadership qualities?
2. Write about someone you consider to be a hero.
3. Write about a famous person you would like to meet. Why would you like to meet this person?

VOCABULARY

ability	dam (n.)	flood (n.)	lower (v.)	request (n.)	unusually
accomplish	debate (n.)	flood (v.)		rescue (n.)	
advise	debate (v.)	formal (adj.)	manner	resident (n.)	various
announce	definite		mission	rise (v.)	
auditorium	delay (v.)	heroine		rush (v.)	war (n.)
	demonstrate	highway	normal		wave (v.)
bridge (n.)	deserve			schedule (v.)	wind (n.)
broadcast (v.)		increase (v.)	official (n.)	service (v.)	
	eliminate	inspire	organize	supply (n.)	
call (n.)	excitement	intelligence			
coincidence	extraordinary		personally	temporary	
communication		leader	present (v.)	topic	
congratulate	fear (n.)	logical	promise (n.)	toward	
controversial	flight	looks			

EXPRESSIONS

to get into an argument
to get into a fight
to shake someone's hand
to save someone's life

to knock down
to be better off
to get things done
to make something ready

He's a man of his word.
We can count on him.
He'll keep his promises.

Don't mention it.
Will it take long?

on that point
in my opinion

DIRECT SPEECH: *Yes/no* Questions	REPORTED SPEECH
I asked Mabel, "Is Sam working this week?"	I asked Mabel if Sam was working that week.
She asked me, "Did you call last night?"	She asked me if I had called the night before.
We asked Sam, "Can you help us tomorrow?"	We asked Sam if he could help us the next day.

DIRECT SPEECH: *Wh-* Questions	REPORTED SPEECH
He asked Nancy, "Where do you live?"	He asked Nancy where she lived.
She asked us, "Who have you spoken to?"	She asked us who we had spoken to.
We asked Fred, "When will you come back?"	We asked Fred when he would come back.

ACTIVE VOICE	PASSIVE VOICE		
		TO BE	Past Participle	
He delivers the mail at ten o'clock.	The mail	is	delivered	at ten o'clock.
The men are building a new bridge.	A new bridge	is being	built.	
They're going to sell that house.	That house	is going to be	sold.	
The people will elect a new mayor.	A new mayor	will be	elected	by the people.
Someone has eaten all the food.	All the food	has been	eaten.	
Nancy wrote that letter.	That letter	was	written	by Nancy.
The girls had left the door open.	The door	had been	left	open.
You can wear jeans anywhere.	Jeans	can be	worn	anywhere.
They should give Otis a chance.	Otis	should be	given	a chance.
We have to save City Park.	City Park	has to be	saved.	

Chapter 4

Lying on a bench in City Park, Soapy moved uneasily. When wild geese begin to fly south to find warm weather, when people start gathering firewood, and when Soapy moves uneasily on his bench in the park, you know that winter is approaching.

A dead leaf fell on Soapy's leg. That was winter's first greeting. Winter is kind to those who sleep on benches in City Park; it gives them a warning before it comes. The north wind reminds the inhabitants of the park that it's time to get ready for the coming cold season. Soapy realized that he would soon have to make preparations for the winter, and therefore he moved uneasily on his bench.

Soapy's ambitions for a winter shelter were not the highest. He had no thought of Caribbean boat trips, of lovely southern skies, or of strolling on a sandy beach by moonlight. Three months in Wakefield Prison was all he desired. Three months of sure bed and board and pleasant company, safe from all those unfriendly police officers, seemed especially desirable to Soapy.

Having decided to go to prison, Soapy began to think about accomplishing his desire. There were easy ways of doing this. The most pleasant way was to dine in luxury at some expensive restaurant; and then after declaring that he could not pay the bill, a police officer would come and take him away. The kind judge of the police court would sentence him to three or more months at Wakefield Prison.

Soapy left his bench and strolled out of the square and across the street to the corner of Broadway and Fifth Avenue. He turned up Broadway and stopped at a brightly lighted restaurant where fashionably dressed people gather every night for fine food and drinks.

Soapy had complete confidence in himself. He was shaved, his coat was decent, and his neat black tie had just been presented to him by a charity worker on Thanksgiving Day. If he could reach a table in the restaurant unsuspected, he would be successful. The part of him that would show above the table would raise no doubt in the waiter's mind. A roast duck, Soapy thought, would be about the right thing—with some fine cheese, a piece of apple pie, and a cup of coffee. The total for his dinner would not be so high as to enrage the restaurant manager, and yet the meal would leave Soapy filled and happy for the journey to his winter home.

But as Soapy stepped inside the restaurant door, the headwaiter's eyes fell on his ragged trousers and worn-out shoes. Strong and ready hands turned him around and pushed him in silence and haste to the sidewalk—and his pleasant thoughts of roast duck faded away.

Soapy turned off Broadway. It seemed that he would not get to prison by filling his stomach in a fancy restaurant. He must think of some other way.

Soapy walked five blocks before he tried again to be arrested. He now saw an opportunity that was sure to succeed. A pleasant-looking young woman was standing in front of a shop window gazing with interest at a display of shoes and dresses. Only a few yards away, a large police officer had stopped to look at his watch.

It was Soapy's idea to pretend to pick up this young woman. Her attractive appearance and the nearness of the "cop" encouraged him to believe that he would soon experience the pleasant feeling of an officer seizing his arm.

Soapy straightened his tie, pushed his hat to a slight angle, and moved toward the woman. He gave a little cough and began to smile. From the corner of his eye he saw that the police officer was watching him. The woman moved away a few steps and continued looking at the shoes and dresses in the shop window. Soapy followed, and stepping to her side he raised his hat and said, "Ah, there, my dear. Would you like to take a walk with me?"

The officer was still watching. All the woman had to do was motion to him, and Soapy would be taken promptly to the police station. The woman faced him and then took hold of his arm.

"Sure," she said happily, "I'll go with you if you buy me a drink."

With the woman holding his arm, Soapy walked past the surprised police officer. At the next corner, however, he left his companion and ran.

When Soapy stopped running, he had reached a well-lighted district with fashionable shops. In a bookstore he noticed a well-dressed man reading a magazine. The man had set his umbrella down near the door. Soapy stepped inside, took the umbrella, and walked away. The man followed hastily.

"My umbrella!" he shouted.

"Oh, is it?" said Soapy rudely. "Well, why don't you call a cop? There's one over there."

The umbrella owner slowed his steps, and Soapy did the same. The police officer looked at the two curiously.

"Well, now, of course," the man said with some uncertainty, "Well—you know how easy it is to make mistakes—I—if it's your umbrella, I hope you'll excuse me. If you recognize it as yours, why—I hope you'll—"

"Of course, it's mine," said Soapy angrily.

The umbrella man left in haste. The police officer hurried to assist a tall woman in a fur coat who was trying to cross the street in front of a bus.

Soapy walked east through a street torn up for improvements. He threw the umbrella away angrily and said some words that were not very nice about officers in blue uniforms. Because he wanted to be arrested, they seemed to regard him as a king who could do no wrong.

At length Soapy reached one of the avenues where there was little activity and not much light. Then he started back toward City Park, for he felt like going home, even if "home" was nothing more than a park bench.

But on an unusually quiet corner, Soapy noticed a quaint little church. A soft light glowed through one of the stained-glass windows, where the organist was practicing the music she was to play the following Sunday morning. From inside the sweet music drifted out to Soapy's ears. He leaned against an old iron fence and listened.

The moon was bright overhead; most vehicles and people had already left the street; birds were making sleepy noises in the trees—and for a little while the peaceful scene seemed like a churchyard in the country. And the music that the organist played held Soapy motionless by the iron fence, for he had known this song in the days when his life contained such things as mothers and roses and friends and clean shirts.

The combination of Soapy's youthful memories and the influence of the little old church made a sudden and wonderful change in his soul. He reviewed in his mind the low depths to which he had fallen—the wasted days, unworthy desires, dead hopes, wrecked opportunities, and lost ambitions that made up his existence.

Also he felt an urge to change his ways. He would pull himself out of the depths to which he had fallen; he would overcome the shameful habits that had taken possession of him. There was still time; he was comparatively young; he would make his dead ambitions come to life again and never let them die. Tomorrow he would go into the busy downtown district and find work. A fish merchant had once offered him a job as a deliveryman. He would look for him tomorrow and ask for a job. He would—

Soapy felt a hand on his arm. He looked quickly around into the broad face of a police officer.

"What are you doing here?" asked the officer.
"Nothing," replied Soapy in all honesty.
"Looks like you're planning to rob one of the houses in this neighborhood, or perhaps this church. Come along with me to the station."

The next morning Soapy stood before the judge in the police court.
"Three months in prison," said the judge, and Soapy was taken away.

STORY QUESTIONS

1. At what time of year does this story take place?
2. How do you know that winter is approaching?
3. Where does Soapy sleep at night?
4. Where did he want to spend the winter? Why?
5. What plan did Soapy have for getting arrested in the restaurant? Why didn't his plan work? Tell what happened.
6. Soapy's second attempt to get arrested involved an attractive young woman. Did things turn out as he expected? Tell what happened.
7. What happened the third time Soapy tried to get arrested? Why didn't the well-dressed man call the police when Soapy took his umbrella?
8. Why is Soapy's attitude toward the police different from the attitude of an average person?
9. Where did Soapy stop on his way back to the park?
10. How did the church music affect Soapy? What did he remember?
11. What did Soapy decide to do with his life?
12. Why did the police officer arrest Soapy?
13. What happened at the police court the next day?
14. Do you feel sorry for Soapy? Why?
15. What would you do if you had no money and no place to sleep?

GROUP WORK • *What should we do about homeless people? Think of some possible solutions and share them with the class.*

• *Wilder Penfield is interviewing Ula Hackey for a popular TV show called "Inside Hollywood." Listen to the interview; then complete the questions below.*

1. _Do you have_ a new boyfriend?

2. Have _____ to Spain?

3. _____ Spanish?

4. How long _____ Antonio?

5. How _____ him?

6. _____ romantic?

7. _____ in love?

8. _____ wedding bells

    _____ future?

9. Why _____ me?

PRACTICE • *What did Mr. Penfield ask Ula Hackey? Change his questions to reported speech.*

1. "Do you have a new boyfriend?" asked Mr. Penfield.
   He asked her if she had a new boyfriend.

WRITTEN EXERCISE • *Complete the sentences using so.*

Sandy wants to visit Paris, _so she can see the Eiffel Tower._

The bandit wore a disguise, _so no one would recognize him._

1. Jane wants to marry a rich man, _____

2. I'll give you my phone number, _____

3. Please speak more slowly, _____

4. Jimmy wants to get good grades, _____

5. Linda wore her prettiest dress to the party, _____

6. Let's meet for coffee, _____

7. Please turn down the radio, _____

8. Sam and Mabel want to live on a farm, _____

9. Mrs. Golo hid her money under the bed, _____

10. Mr. Poole is being nice to his wife, _____

Listen and practice.

GROUP WORK • *Now it's your turn to play "The Dating Game." You can ask the following questions or make up your own questions.*

1. If I were sitting alone in a cafe and you wanted to meet me, what would you do?
2. Give me the title of a pop song that describes our first date together.
3. If you were a talking alarm clock, what would you say in the morning to wake me up?
4. Let's say I'm the manager of a loan company. If I loaned you a lot of money, what would you do with it?
5. With the barter system, I give you something and you give me something of equal value or better. If I gave you my pet tarantula, what would you give me?
6. Let's say I'm the manager of an employment agency that only handles weird jobs. What weird job would you really like to have?

PAIR WORK • *Have conversations similar to the examples. Student B uses **so** or **neither** to show agreement with Student A.*

A: **I like "The Dating Game."**	B: **So do I.**
A: **I've never been to Disneyland.**	B: **Neither have I.**

1. A: I'm thirsty. B: _____.
2. A: I'd like a cold drink. B: _____.
3. A: I'm not very hungry. B: _____.
4. A: I don't want anything to eat. B: _____.
5. A: I got up early this morning. B: _____.
6. A: I didn't sleep much last night. B: _____.
7. A: I've been very busy recently. B: _____.
8. A: I shouldn't work so hard. B: _____.
9. A: I won't be here tomorrow. B: _____.
10. A: I'm going to a party. B: _____.

WRITTEN EXERCISE • *Complete the sentences using the correct form of the verb in parentheses.*

They want us ___*to bring*___ some paper. (bring)

I don't remember them ___*using*___ the copy machine. (use)

1. He asked them _____ the building. (leave)
2. She's worried about him _____ in trouble. (get)
3. They object to us _____ a new car. (buy)
4. I expect you _____ home early. (come)
5. He invited her _____ a movie. (see)
6. She's responsible for him _____ the job. (get)
7. They told us _____ at the office at nine o'clock. (be)
8. I'm tired of you _____ all the time. (complain)
9. We object to her _____ at night. (work)

WRITTEN EXERCISE • *Complete the sentences using **feel, look, smell,** and **taste** with appropriate adjectives. You can use the adjectives in the box, or any adjectives you wish. There can be more than one appropriate adjective for each sentence.*

delicious	dry	great	sour	tired
depressed	fresh	hard	terrible	uncomfortable
disgusting	funny	lovely	tight	wonderful

This lemonade **tastes** sour. 1.

My hair **feels** dry. 2.

Nick looks depressed. 3.

These fish **smell** fresh. 4.

This soup… 5.

This dress… 6.

You… 7.

These flowers… 8.

This food… 9.

This bed… 10.

Your hat… 11.

That cigar smoke… 12.

Listen and practice.

Rosie Bloom is having a party. Her guests are all giving her compliments.

GROUP WORK 1 • *Imagine you are at a party. One student is the host or hostess. Other students are the guests. Each guest says something complimentary to the host or hostess about:*

1. his/her appearance
2. the house
3. the food
4. the music
5. the way the host/hostess dances
6. the other guests at the party

Use the short conversations on page 70 as models.

PAIR WORK • *Listen to actors read the criticisms in column A and the ways of rejecting criticism in column B. Then practice these sentences with a partner.*

A
1. That's an ugly tie you have on.
2. You look horrible in that dress.
3. You certainly have bad taste.
4. I don't like your new hairdo.
5. I can't stand the way you dance.
6. What an ugly house!
7. You're a lousy host.
8. This food tastes awful.
9. This is the worst party I've ever been to.

B
I'm sorry you don't like it.
What an awful thing to say!
Look who's talking.
Who cares what you think!
That's too bad.
Who asked you?
Don't give me that.
So don't eat it.
Why don't you leave, then?

GROUP WORK 2 • *One student is the host or hostess at a party. Other students are the guests. Each student says something critical to the host or hostess about the house, the food, the music, and so on. The host or hostess responds to each criticism in an appropriate manner.*

WRITTEN EXERCISE • *Complete the sentences with a suitable adjective or adverb.*

The Bascombs live (comfortable) *more comfortably* than the Browns.
Mr. Bascomb is the (ambitious) *most ambitious* man in town.
He works (hard) *harder* than anyone I've ever met.

1. Barbara smiles (easy) _____ than Anne.
2. Barbara is one of the (friendly) _____ people I know.
3. My dog is (big) _____ and (smart) _____ than yours.
4. I have the (good) _____ dog in the world.
5. Tino exercises (regular) _____ and always takes his vitamins.
6. He is in (good) _____ shape than most people.
7. Nancy doesn't dress as (fashionable) _____ as Maria.
8. Maria wears the (beautiful) _____ clothes you've ever seen.
9. She dresses so (good) _____ that she looks like a movie star.
10. Mona gets up (early) _____ than Fred.
11. She is (busy) _____ and (energetic) _____ than he is.
12. Fred is one of the (lazy) _____ people around.

Listen and practice.

Linda often sees her boyfriend Joe after school. Today they are meeting at Dimple's for a soda.

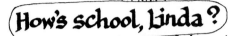

1.

How's school, Linda?

Fine. Only one semester to go.

What are you going to do after you graduate?

Well, I'd like to go into fashion, you know, designing women's clothes.

2.

You dress so well—I'm sure you'll make a great designer.

Thanks, Joe. What do you plan to do?

I don't know. The only thing I'm good at is baseball.

3.

Have you ever thought of becoming a professional baseball player?

No, it seems like an impossible dream. The competition is so tough. Maybe I'm not good enough.

Don't say that. I've seen you play and I know how good you are. You just have to believe in yourself.

4.

Do you really think I could make it as a pro?

Sure. But you'll never know unless you try.

You're right. I just needed some encouragement. I think I'll go for it.

GROUP WORK • *Discuss what it takes to become:*

a politician	a teacher	a singer
a basketball player	a mechanic	an actor
a film director	a lawyer	a police officer

PAIR WORK 1 • *Discuss your plans for the future, including career goals. Student A seems discouraged about his or her future. Student B tries to encourage Student A. Use some of the sentences below in your discussion.*

STUDENT A

It's so hard.
Maybe I'm not good enough.
There's so much competition.
I'm not sure I can do it.

STUDENT B

Come on, you can do it.
You have what it takes.
Don't give up.
You'll never know unless you try.

PAIR WORK 2 • *Student A asks questions. Student B answers using* **had never . . . before.**

A: Did the girls enjoy riding their bicycles in the park?
B: **Yes, they had never ridden their bicycles in the park before.**

1. Did Barney enjoy dancing with Mona last night?
2. Did Linda enjoy playing tennis with Joe yesterday?
3. Did the children enjoy going to the circus?
4. Did Fred enjoy listening to classical music?
5. Did Maria enjoy seeing a Russian movie?
6. Did your friends enjoy staying at the Plaza Hotel?
7. Did Barbara enjoy driving a sports car?
8. Did Mr. Bascomb enjoy wearing cowboy boots?

WRITTEN EXERCISE • *Add an explanation to each of the remarks below. Use your imagination.*

Jenny is very happy. _Her basketball team won the championship._
OR _She got an A on her final exam._

1. I feel sorry for those people. _____
2. I don't believe anything that man says. _____
3. My neighbor has a serious problem. _____
4. I'm disappointed in you. _____
5. You shouldn't eat so much candy. _____
6. I hate to take the bus. _____
7. Could you loan me ten dollars? _____
8. I've got to run now. _____

Listen and practice.

PAIR WORK • *Have similar conversations. Student A is selling the items shown above at the swap meet. Student B is a customer who wants to get a good price on one of those items.*

PRACTICE • *Change the sentences using the passive form.*

> They <u>sold</u> the house last week.
> **The house was sold last week.**

> I'm glad someone <u>repaired</u> the gate.
> **I'm glad the gate was repaired.**

1. I'm surprised they <u>offered</u> my sister a job at the hotel.
2. She didn't know that the management <u>expected</u> her to work overtime.
3. She complained and the management <u>accused</u> her of being lazy.
4. When she did some extra work, no one <u>paid</u> her for it.
5. They <u>treated</u> her terribly.
6. Someone <u>called</u> her a trouble-maker.
7. They <u>warned</u> her not to say anything.
8. Yesterday the management <u>told</u> her to look for another job.

PAIR WORK 1 • *Student A reads the sentences, which are about various characters in this book, and asks the question, "What does he (she) wish?" Student B makes a logical conclusion about each character.*

> A: Mr. Poole went to the Magnolia Restaurant last night. He didn't enjoy it because the food and service were terrible. What does he wish?
>
> B: **He wishes he hadn't gone to the Magnolia Restaurant last night.**
> OR **He wishes he had gone somewhere else for dinner.**

1. Barney ate a lot of candy when he was a boy. Now he has bad teeth.
2. Anne didn't think she would need her umbrella this morning. But on her way to work, it started raining and she got all wet.
3. Linda stayed up very late last night. Today she's tired and sleepy.
4. Fred forgot to take out the trash. Now his kitchen is full of flies.
5. Nick was sick yesterday, but he went to work anyway. Today he feels worse.
6. Last month Fred turned down a good job at the post office. Since then he hasn't been able to find another job.
7. Barbara didn't eat breakfast before going to work. Now she's very hungry.
8. Jane's friends went to a wonderful party Saturday night. Jane didn't go with them, and now she's sorry.
9. Jack loved Millie, but he didn't marry her. Now he's unhappy.

PAIR WORK 2 • *In this exercise your partner says something to you. You believe it is the opposite of what he or she said before. You have to answer **I thought you said . . .***

> A: Mom's Cafe is expensive.
> B: **I thought you said it wasn't expensive.**

> A: The boys went to the park.
> B: **I thought you said they didn't go to the park.**

> A: I'll be home tomorrow.
> B: **I thought you said you wouldn't be home tomorrow.**

1. Ben Dole is a good businessman.
2. He works very hard.
3. He has a girlfriend.
4. He wants to get married.
5. He's going to buy a house.
6. He can get a loan from the bank.
7. He talked with Mr. Bascomb.
8. Mr. Bascomb likes Ben.
9. He'll help Ben.
10. Nancy likes to travel.
11. She's very adventurous.
12. She wants to visit Panama.
13. She'll go there next year.
14. Panama is a tropical country.
15. The people are very friendly.
16. Nancy has friends in Panama.
17. She can speak Spanish.
18. She learned Spanish in school.

FREE RESPONSE

1. What would you do if you were sitting in a movie theater and the people in front of you were talking?
2. What kinds of things irritate you?
3. Do you remember the last time you lost your temper?
4. Do you spend much time alone? What do you think about when you're alone?
5. How often do you see your friends? Where do you go? What do you do?
6. Have you made any important decisions lately?
7. What is the smartest thing you've ever done? Or the dumbest thing?
8. How do you feel about the future: optimistic or pessimistic? Why?
9. Do you have any predictions for next year?
10. What would you like to see happen in the future?

VOCABULARY

alarm clock	desirable	hostess	semester
angel	desire (v.)		shameful
assist (v.)	district	influence (n.)	shelter
			soul
bouquet	enrage	journey	southern
broad	equal		stroll
	existence	merchant	
castle		motion (v.)	title
charity	fancy		total
companion	fashionable	northern	tough
competition			
complete (adj.)	gorgeous	preparation	unfriendly
compliment (n.)	greeting	pretend	
cough (v.)	guy	princess	vehicle
dead	hairdo	regard (v.)	warning
decent	honesty	review (v.)	wasted
declare	hope (n.)	rudely	weird

EXPRESSIONS

He left in haste.
He felt an urge to change his ways.
Some guys will stop at nothing.
How much do you want for it?

It's very becoming.
You have good taste.
You're so sweet.
What a beautiful house.

Nope.
Take it or leave it.
It's a deal.
It's nothing, really.

Who cares?
Who asked you?
Don't give me that.
Look who's talking.

Oh, come on.
Go for it.
Are you serious?
Tell you what . . .

to pick up

1. Mr. Bascomb is a rich man.

   He has _____ money.
   A. many   C. a little
   B. plenty   D. a lot of

2. He is very busy. He doesn't have

   _____ free time.
   A. many   C. no
   B. much   D. some

3. We drank most of the coffee. There's only

   _____ left.
   A. many   C. a little
   B. a few   D. a lot

4. How _____ is the park from here?
   A. long   C. close
   B. much   D. far

5. Anyone can ride a bicycle.

   It's _____.
   A. easy   C. hard
   B. difficult   D. funny

6. Jack walks _____ when he is tired.
   A. fast   C. slowly
   B. slow   D. quickly

7. _____ are you going?
   To a movie.
   A. Why   C. How
   B. Where   D. When

8. _____ is the name of the movie?
   A Fool in Love.
   A. Who   C. What
   B. How   D. Which

9. _____ do you want to see *A Fool in Love?*
   Because Ula Hackey is starring in it.
   A. Why   C. When
   B. Who   D. Where

10. She is a famous actress. Everyone knows

    _____ she is.
    A. which   C. where
    B. who   D. how

11. You like Miss Hackey very much,

    _____?
    A. do you   C. don't you
    B. you do   D. you don't

12. You haven't met her, _____?
    A. have you   C. haven't you
    B. you have   D. you haven't

13. You are too timid. You should be more

    _____.
    A. polite   C. strong
    B. pleasant   D. aggressive

14. We hoped Peter _____ give us a
    ride downtown.
    A. will   C. would
    B. can   D. should

15. If only I _____ drive a car.
    A. can   C. will
    B. could   D. would

16. Sam and Mabel would like to live

    _____ a farm.
    A. on   C. at
    B. in   D. to

17. We saw a dog _____ our
    backyard.
    A. on   C. at
    B. in   D. to

18. The dog jumped _____ the fence.
    A. with   C. under
    B. around   D. over

19. Otis took Gloria _____ Mom's
    Cafe for lunch.
    A. on   C. at
    B. in   D. to

20. Mom's Cafe is known _____ good
    food.
    A. for   C. from
    B. of   D. with

21. Fred and Barney _____ to Bear Lake last Friday.
    - A. drive
    - B. are driving
    - C. drove
    - D. have driven

22. They often _____ to Bear Lake in the summer.
    - A. go
    - B. are going
    - C. were going
    - D. have gone

23. They _____ for three days, but so far they have only caught one fish.
    - A. fish
    - B. are fishing
    - C. fishing
    - D. have been fishing

24. They would have more success if they _____ a boat.
    - A. rent
    - B. are renting
    - C. rented
    - D. have rented

25. Look! Fred _____ a big fish!
    - A. holds
    - B. is holding
    - C. held
    - D. has held

26. He caught that fish while Barney _____.
    - A. sleeps
    - B. is sleeping
    - C. was sleeping
    - D. has slept

27. He will show the fish to his sister when he _____ home.
    - A. gets
    - B. will get
    - C. got
    - D. has gotten

28. Fred is smiling. He _____ be very happy.
    - A. might
    - B. must
    - C. can
    - D. would

29. Hurry up! I'm afraid we _____ be late for work.
    - A. will
    - B. would
    - C. can
    - D. must

30. You work too hard. You _____ relax more.
    - A. will
    - B. shall
    - C. would
    - D. should

31. Sandy felt bad because her friend didn't call her _____ write to her.
    - A. and
    - B. but
    - C. or
    - D. so

32. Yesterday the weather was terrible, _____ today it's beautiful.
    - A. but
    - B. because
    - C. so
    - D. although

33. Mabel didn't finish the housework _____ she had lots of time.
    - A. or
    - B. because
    - C. so
    - D. although

34. Jack doesn't like rock music, _____ he never goes to discotheques.
    - A. but
    - B. because
    - C. so
    - D. although

35. Come here. There's _____ I have to tell you.
    - A. something
    - B. anything
    - C. nothing
    - D. everything

36. You can help some people, but you can't help _____.
    - A. someone
    - B. anyone
    - C. no one
    - D. everyone

37. Linda can't go _____ tonight because she has to study.
    - A. somewhere
    - B. anywhere
    - C. no where
    - D. everywhere

38. We are all broke. _____ of us has any money.
    - A. Both
    - B. Either
    - C. One
    - D. None

39. My dog is _____ than yours.
    - A. smart
    - B. more smart
    - C. smarter
    - D. more smarter

40. Tino is the _____ person I've ever met.
    - A. happier
    - B. happiest
    - C. more happy
    - D. most happiest

41. I wish you _____ the concert last Friday.

    A. attend   C. have attended
    B. attended   D. had attended

42. I'll never understand why _____ classical music.

    A. you not like   C. don't you like
    B. you don't like   D. can't you like

43. The bank _____ held up yesterday.

    A. is   C. has
    B. was   D. has been

44. My car is still at the garage. It _____ repaired yet.

    A. wasn't   C. won't be
    B. hasn't   D. hasn't been

45. Why did Gloria let the cat _____ on the sofa?

    A. sleep   C. sleeping
    B. to sleep   D. slept

46. Miss Hackey said, "I've done everything." What did she say?

    She said she _____ everything.

    A. does   C. done
    B. did   D. had done

47. "Do you want a soda, Bob?" asked Jane. What did she ask him?

    She asked him if he _____ a soda.

    A. wants   C. has wanted
    B. wanted   D. ever wanted

48. "Why are you crying, Anne?" asked Johnnie. What did he ask her?

    He asked her why she _____.

    A. cries   C. was crying
    B. is crying   D. has been crying

49. I can't hear the radio very well.

    Would you please turn it _____?
    A. on   C. up
    B. off   D. down

50. We can't use the computer. _____.

    A. It isn't working
    B. It's unemployed
    C. It doesn't make sense
    D. It's out of this world

Chapter 5

TOPICS

Adventure

Travel

GRAMMAR

Third conditional

Perfect modals

FUNCTIONS

Expressing past advisability

Expressing regret

Expressing possibility in the past

Making logical conclusions

Giving opinions

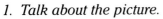
1. Talk about the picture.
2. Listen to the story.
3. Answer the story questions.

READING

Last Sunday, Otis Jackson held a picnic at City Park. He had organized it as part of his campaign to save the park. There were lots of games, contests, and refreshments and, best of all, the picnic was free. The festivities began with Otis giving a short, five-minute speech in defense of the park. After the speech, Otis announced the day's activities, which included a pie-eating contest and a sack race.

The first event, the pie-eating contest, ended in a tie between Fred and Barney. Both men were able to eat six lemon pies. Barney said he would have won if he hadn't gotten an upset stomach. As for Fred, he would have done better if he had listened to his sister. She had told him to skip breakfast that morning so he would be really hungry for the pie-eating contest. If he had taken her advice, he probably would have won.

The sack race was very exciting, with Jenny Lassiter winning by less than a yard over Marty Mango. Marty was ahead and would have won if he hadn't fallen just before the finish line. There were many other activities for children and adults, but of all the attractions, the most popular was Simon Gamer's magic show. He astonished and amazed everyone with his card tricks and disappearing acts. It seemed he could make almost anything disappear with his magic wand. And his card tricks were so clever that no one could figure out how he did them.

After Simon's magic show everyone got together and sang. Anne would certainly have led the singing if she had been at the picnic. But she was busy making preparations for her trip to Hollywood and couldn't spare the time. Johnnie would have enjoyed the picnic much more if Anne had been there. He wished that Simon could have used his magic wand to make her appear. He missed Anne more than he liked to admit. All the other people there were enjoying themselves so much that the picnic would have gone on all afternoon if it hadn't suddenly started to rain. Well, it was fun while it lasted.

1. Why did Otis decide to hold a free picnic at City Park last Sunday?
2. Who won the pie-eating contest?
3. What would have happened if Barney hadn't gotten an upset stomach?
4. Why did Fred's sister tell him not to eat breakfast that morning?
5. What would have happened if he had taken her advice?
6. Who won the sack race?
7. What would have happened if Marty hadn't fallen just before the finish line?
8. What was the most popular attraction at the picnic?
9. What could Simon do with his magic wand?
10. Why didn't Anne come to the picnic?
11. Would Johnnie have enjoyed the picnic more if Anne had been there?
12. What did Johnnie wish?

THIRD CONDITIONAL

Marty would have won the sack race if he hadn't fallen before the finish line.
Johnnie would have enjoyed the picnic much more if Anne had been there.

The if-clause states an action that did not take place in the past. However, if the action in the if-clause had actually taken place, it is quite probable that the action in the result clause would have taken place too. We use the third conditional to talk about what might have happened.

Listen and practice.

SAM: Are you enjoying the picnic, Linda?

LINDA: I sure am, especially the magic show. Simon just made a rabbit disappear with his wand.

SAM: That's nothing! I just saw Albert make five hot dogs disappear, all by himself.

LINDA: Here comes Albert now. He doesn't look very well.

ALBERT: Oh, I've never felt so bad in all my life. If only I'd known, I wouldn't have eaten that last hot dog.

LINDA: Oh, Albert, look at you! You've eaten so much you can hardly stand up.

ALBERT: Come on, Linda, you're supposed to eat at picnics. And what's wrong with me being a little overweight? After all, we can't all be as athletic as Tino or dance as well as Peter.

LINDA: You're just making excuses, Albert. Everyone knows you have the biggest appetite in Wickam City. If you had entered the pie-eating contest, you would have won it easily.

ALBERT: If they had served apple pie instead of lemon pie, I would have entered. Lemon pie makes me very thirsty.

LINDA: Albert, you've got to get your mind off food. Look at Johnnie. He reads good books and tries to improve himself. All you think about is eating.

ALBERT: Well, if I had known how much it bothered you, I would have tried to change.

LINDA: It takes a lot of determination and sacrifice, Albert. Maybe you aren't up to it. Look, why don't we just drop the whole thing?

ALBERT: Not at all. I'm going to diet this very minute. I'm going to start reading some good books, and you're going to teach me how to dance.

LINDA: Oh, Albert, that's wonderful! I could kiss you.

ALBERT: Well, now that that's settled, let's celebrate the new me. I could sure use a big hamburger with French fries and a malt. How about you?

LINDA: Oh, Albert!

WRITTEN EXERCISE • *Complete the sentences using the third conditional.*

Johnnie _would have enjoyed_ the picnic much more if Anne ___ *had been* ___ there.
(enjoy) (be)

Marty ___ *would have won* ___ the race if he *hadn't fallen* just before the finish line.
(win) (not fall)

1. Fred _____ the pie-eating contest if he _____ to his
   (win)   (listen)
   sister.

2. Linda _____ the dishes if she _____ in a hurry.
   (wash)   (not be)

3. Barney _____ his keys if he _____ in the right place.
   (find)   (look)

4. Gloria _____ to work on time if she _____ the bus.
   (get)   (not miss)

5. We _____ you if we _____ your telephone number.
   (call)   (have)

6. Sandy _____ to the party if she _____ invited.
   (go)   (be)

7. She _____ Tom if she _____ to the party.
   (meet)   (go)

8. Barbara _____ the movie if it _____ a happy ending.
   (like)   (have)

9. Tino _____ to wash the car if Barbara _____ him.
   (forget)   (not remind)

1. Talk about the picture.
2. Listen to the story.
3. Answer the story questions.

Johnnie Wilson has been feeling very depressed. He is secretly in love with Anne Jones, but she acts as if he didn't exist. It seems she is only interested in going to Hollywood and starting a career as a professional singer. For several days Johnnie has been trying to see Anne. He must have called her apartment at least a dozen times this week, but she refused to answer the phone. She didn't want to have any more arguments with Johnnie about her decision to become a singer.

Johnnie thought everything would be OK if he could just talk to Anne. Then he could make her change her mind about going to Hollywood. But it was no use; she kept avoiding him. Johnnie had almost given up trying to see her when his opportunity finally came. Last night there was an amateur singing contest at the Disco Club and Anne was one of the contestants.

When Johnnie arrived at the Disco Club, it was ten o'clock and the contest was almost over. There were only two contestants who hadn't sung yet, Olivia Palmer and Anne Jones. Olivia came on stage first. She didn't have a very good voice but her boyfriend, Barry Craxton, thought she was terrific. He started clapping before she had even finished her song. The big guy must have clapped for five minutes without stopping. Johnnie was irritated, but he didn't say anything. He was anxious to see Anne. When she finally walked on stage, he could feel his heart pounding.

Anne smiled at the audience and then started singing one of Johnnie's favorite tunes. He thought she had a beautiful voice and was sure to win first prize. Anne was only halfway through her song, however, when someone in the audience started booing. It was Barry Craxton, the same person who had been clapping so hard just a few minutes earlier. Johnnie was very upset. He was about to complain to the manager when suddenly Barry threw a tomato at Anne.

The tomato struck Anne on the shoulder. Johnnie was so mad he ran up to Barry and challenged him to a fight. The big man looked down at Johnnie, who was only half his size, and started laughing. Johnnie drew back his fist and hit Barry on the chin. Then Barry grabbed Johnnie by the neck and started choking him. Suddenly, a guitar came crashing down on Barry's head. Anne had come running over from the stage and was now in the fight. She couldn't just stand by and watch Johnnie get beaten up without trying to help.

The fight ended quickly with Barry being thrown out of the club by the manager. Johnnie didn't get hurt, but his glasses were broken. He should have taken them off before fighting Barry. Anne didn't have much luck, either. She was disqualified from the contest for taking part in the fight. It was announced that a local singer, Alberta Black, had won first prize.

1. Why has Johnnie been feeling depressed?
2. Why did Anne refuse to answer Johnnie's telephone calls?
3. How did he finally get an opportunity to see her?
4. Who were the last two women to compete in the singing contest?
5. Who stood up and clapped for Olivia?
6. Why did Johnnie get into a fight with Barry?
7. What did Anne do?
8. What did the manager do?
9. What happened to Anne as a result of the fight?
10. Do you think Anne should have stayed out of the fight? Why?

PRACTICE 1 • *Make sentences using **should have.***

> Anne felt bad because she didn't win the singing contest.
> **She should have won the singing contest.**
>
> She lost the contest because she didn't finish her song.
> **She should have finished her song.**

1. Marty failed the test because he didn't study.
2. He got in trouble because he didn't go home after school.
3. Linda couldn't go to the party because she didn't finish her homework.
4. You didn't hear about the party because you didn't come to the last meeting.
5. Fred didn't get the job because he didn't wear a suit and tie to the interview.
6. He couldn't get a loan because he didn't pay his bills.
7. Gloria got wet because she didn't take her umbrella when she left the house.
8. Albert got a stomachache because he ate five hot dogs.

PRACTICE 2 • *Make sentences using **shouldn't have.***

> Anne was disqualified because she left the stage.
> **She shouldn't have left the stage.**
>
> Johnnie's glasses were broken because he got into a fight with Barry.
> **He shouldn't have gotten into a fight with Barry.**

1. Peter is embarrassed because he forgot Maria's birthday.
2. Gladys is broke because she spent all her money on perfume.
3. Marty got in trouble because he talked back to his mother.
4. Spike went to jail because he robbed a bank.
5. Mona didn't get much sleep because she went to bed late.
6. Bertha is unhappy because she married Stanley.
7. Mr. Farley was late to work because he stopped for coffee at Mom's Cafe.
8. He almost lost his job because he made fun of the boss.

GROUP WORK • *Think of something you did or didn't do that you regret. Tell the others what happened. What do you think you should have done or shouldn't have done in that situation? Find out what the others would have done in your place.*

🎧 *Listen and practice.*

ANNE: You shouldn't have started that fight, Johnnie. You might have been hurt.

JOHNNIE: Come on, that guy was trying to make you lose the contest. He's the one who threw the tomato. I couldn't just stand there and let him get away with it.

ANNE: Maybe not, but you could have handled it differently.

JOHNNIE: What do you mean?

ANNE: You could have called the manager. You didn't have to start fighting. Now look at your glasses! They're broken.

JOHNNIE: Don't worry about my glasses. If you hadn't left the stage, you might have won the contest.

ANNE: It doesn't matter. It's just a silly amateur contest. I'm more concerned about doing well in Hollywood. That's where the real competition takes place.

JOHNNIE: I can't figure you out. You had a good, secure job at the bank. Now you want to gamble everything on a singing career.

ANNE: My job at the bank was unbearable, Johnnie. I couldn't have stood it another day.

JOHNNIE: You should have come to me. I might have been able to help you. I could have spoken to Mr. Bascomb.

ANNE: It wouldn't have made any difference. Don't you see? My mind is made up. I'm going to be a professional singer.

JOHNNIE: You're so stubborn, Anne. Don't you realize how hard it is to make it in Hollywood?

ANNE: Johnnie, why are you being so negative? I thought you were on my side.

JOHNNIE: I am on your side. I just want to make sure you know what you're doing, that's all.

ANNE: There must be something else. Every time I mention Hollywood you get upset. What is it you want, Johnnie?

JOHNNIE: Oh, Anne, can't you see? I want you to stay here, with me.

ANNE: But why?

JOHNNIE: Well . . . because I . . . I'm in love with you. I've been in love with you for a long time. But I've kept it secret until now.

ANNE: Oh, Johnnie, you should have told me before. It might have made a difference.

JOHNNIE: But now it's too late. Is that what you're saying?

ANNE: I'm afraid so. I've already told everyone I'm going to Hollywood. If I don't go now, people will say it's because I don't have the nerve.

JOHNNIE: Does it really matter what people think?

ANNE: Probably not. But this is something I've always wanted to do. Don't you understand?

JOHNNIE: Sure, I understand. Your career is more important to you than I am. You don't really care about me.

ANNE: That isn't true, Johnnie. I'm really very fond of you. It's just that I have to prove something.

JOHNNIE: Well, I guess there's nothing more I can say. Good-bye, Anne.

ANNE: Good-bye, Johnnie. Take care.

WRITTEN EXERCISE • *Complete the sentences using **could have** + past participle.*

Johnnie didn't have to go to the Disco Club last night. He _could have stayed_ home.
(stay)

He didn't have to get into a fight with Barry. He _could have called_ the manager.
(call)

1. Mabel didn't have to stay home this afternoon. She _____ to a movie.
(go)

2. She didn't have to do the ironing. She _____ someone to do it.
(pay)

3. Gloria didn't have to take the bus to work. She _____ a ride.
(get)

4. She didn't have to eat lunch in a restaurant. She _____ her lunch.
(take)

5. Bruno didn't have to become a mechanic. He _____ something else.
(do)

6. He didn't have to work at the garage. He _____ another job.
(find)

7. Ed didn't have to eat pizza for dinner. He _____ spaghetti.
(have)

8. He didn't have to watch TV after dinner. He _____ a book.
(read)

PAIR WORK • *Have conversations similar to the examples.*

A: Do you think Nick went to the bank?
B: I don't know. He **might have gone** there.

A: Do you think he talked to Mr. Bascomb?
B: I don't know. He **might have talked** to him.

A: Do you think he got the loan he wanted?
B: I don't know. He **might have gotten** it.

1. Do you think Marty took the magazines that were on Mrs. Golo's desk?
2. Do you think he went to Jenny's house?
3. Do you think he gave her the magazines?
4. Do you think Otis saw his picture in the newspaper this morning?
5. Do you think he read the article that was written about him?
6. Do you think Suzi Suzuki wrote the article?
7. Do you think he told her about his plans for the campaign?
8. Do you think Peter got the note Maria sent him?
9. Do you think he called her?

"If only I'd known, I wouldn't have gone," Peter was saying to Nick Vitakis. Peter had taken his car to Nick's garage to get gas, and Nick had been anxious to hear about Peter's recent trip to the South Pacific. While they were talking, Barney drove up with Dr. Pasto in the back seat of his taxi. Soon they were all listening attentively while Peter told his story. They all enjoyed hearing about Peter's trips, and Nick would have given anything to go to the South Pacific. Barney thought he was already an expert on that part of the world because he had seen so many travel films. Dr. Pasto had been all over the South Pacific when he was a young man and was interested to know how it had changed.

"But Peter," Barney asked, "how is it that you're able to take all these interesting trips to exotic, faraway places?" Barney knew that Peter was always traveling and that he had already been to Europe, South America, and Asia several times.

"It's my import-export business, Barney," answered Peter. "I often go to foreign countries to buy art objects and have them shipped to the United States. And I always take advantage of the opportunity to combine business with pleasure."

"But you were saying that if you had known something you wouldn't have taken the trip," said Nick. "What happened? Didn't it turn out the way you expected?"

"No, not at all," replied Peter. "First of all, the plane was several hours late taking off. The weather was rough and the food was bad, and when we were about eighty miles from Zorapunga, our destination, we ran into a heavy tropical storm. Our pilot lost radio contact with the airport and flew off course. We were forced to make a crash landing in the mountains north of Zorapunga."

"Peter! You might have died!" exclaimed Nick. "Couldn't you have landed at sea, or something like that?"

"We could have, Nick," replied Peter, "if Zorapunga weren't so far inland. It's a long way from the sea. Besides, the plane didn't have any life rafts."

"Well, you could have jumped," said Dr. Pasto. "A parachute landing is always safer than going down with the plane."

"We would have jumped, Dr. Pasto, if there had been any parachutes in good condition. When we tried them on, we found they'd been chewed full of holes by rats. I should never have taken one of those cheap flights."

"What happened next, Peter?" Barney was so nervous he was biting his nails.

"By a miracle we all survived the crash, but the airplane caught fire and was totally destroyed. We had no maps, no food, and no water. The copilot said he knew the area and would lead us to civilization. He started out, leading us down the mountain and through the jungle. I would have had more confidence in him, though, if he'd been about a foot taller. He was so short that he couldn't see over the top of the jungle grass. After two days and nights of steady walking, we came back to the plane. We had been walking in circles. We were hopelessly lost."

"You should have had a compass," said Nick.

"If I had planned on a crash landing in the middle of the jungle, I would have taken one," said Peter. "As it was, our situation was desperate. We were suffering from hunger and thirst, and we hadn't slept a wink for two days and nights. We were trying to decide what to do when suddenly we were surrounded by tall, powerfully built natives. They spoke a language we couldn't understand. They motioned to us to follow them, and we were in no position to refuse."

"It sounds just like when I was in the South Pacific as a young man," said Dr. Pasto. "I wish I could have been there to see it."

"Not me," said Barney. "I'd rather see it at the movies. But what happened next, Peter?"

"They took us to a small village hidden high in the mountain jungle. You should have seen the view. It was beautiful! They motioned to us to sit down and then brought us a delicious dinner of roast pig. After the meal we were very tired and they led us to a large grass hut. We fell asleep immediately, in spite of the lions roaring in the distance. In the morning we woke up to the sound of jungle drums. The natives took us from the hut and led us to a group of large black iron pots full of water. They made us take off our clothes and get into the pots. Then they lit fires under the pots and the water began to get hotter and hotter."

"Oh, no," exclaimed Nick. "Cannibals!"

"That's funny," remarked Dr. Pasto, "I don't remember there being cannibals in that region. How did you escape, Peter?"

"I would have run if I'd been able to, but there were too many of them. There was no chance of escape. Just when I was sure that I was going to die, they brought us soap, washcloths, and towels. One of them spoke to me in fluent English. 'You'll feel much better after a nice hot bath, my friend. Don't worry about your clothes. They're being washed now.' He smiled and shook my hand. 'Welcome to the Authentic Jungle View Hotel.'"

"Incredible," said Barney. "You were saved! All your troubles were over."

"No, Barney," answered Peter. "The worst was yet to come. After the bath we had a delicious breakfast of fresh tropical fruit. Then the native guide explained to us that the huts had been reserved by a tour group arriving that night from Texas. He said he would lead us all down the mountain to where a bus would take us to Zorapunga. Then came the bad news."

"What was that, Peter?" asked Dr. Pasto.

"When I saw the bill for one night's lodging, with hot bath and meals included, I could have fainted. It was more expensive than the best hotel in Wickam City."

1. Where did Peter go on his last trip?
2. What caused the plane to fly off course?
3. What happened to the airplane after it crashed into the mountains?
4. What happened when the copilot tried to lead Peter and the others to safety?
5. Why was their situation desperate?
6. What happened as they were trying to decide what to do?
7. Where did the natives take Peter and his friends?
8. What happened in the morning that scared Peter?
9. Why didn't he try to escape?
10. What finally happened to Peter and his friends?
11. What do you think of Peter's adventure?
12. Have you ever had an exciting adventure?

GROUP WORK • *Talk about your favorite adventure stories. Who were the heroes of these stories? What dangerous situations did they get into? Share the best story with the class.*

PRACTICE 1 • *Make sentences using the third conditional.*

The pilot lost radio contact and flew off course.
If he hadn't lost radio contact, he wouldn't have flown off course.

He made a crash landing and the plane was destroyed.
If he hadn't made a crash landing, the plane wouldn't have been destroyed.

1. She got coffee on her dress and had to change it.
2. She missed the bus and was late to work.
3. She was in a hurry and forgot her umbrella.
4. It rained and she got wet.
5. She lost her temper and threw her handbag in the air.
6. It fell in the gutter and got lost.
7. She needed money and asked her brother for a loan.
8. He was a nice guy and gave her the money.
9. She was grateful and thanked him.

PRACTICE 2 • *Make sentences using **must have**.*

Sam was unhappy because he had lost his watch. Now he is smiling.
He must have found his watch.

There isn't any food in the refrigerator. Mabel has just left the house with her shopping bag.
She must have gone to the market.

1. There were some cookies in the dish a little while ago. They are all gone now and Albert has cookie crumbs on his shirt.
2. Jimmy said he wouldn't watch TV until he finished his homework. He's watching TV now.
3. Barbara and Tino have just played a hard game of tennis. Barbara looks very happy.
4. Mr. Bascomb loves his wife and only complains when she gives him chicken and peas for dinner. He's complaining now.
5. Nancy promised to show us her new camera today. Here she comes now, but she doesn't have the camera.

WRITTEN EXERCISE • *Complete the sentences using* ***should have****,* ***must have****, or* ***might have****.*

I was late to work this morning. I ___*should have left*___ the house earlier.
(leave)

Anne didn't go home after work. She ___*might have gone*___ to the park or the library.
(go)

Mr. Bascomb is very tired. He ___*must have worked*___ hard today.
(work)

1. Jenny said Otis's picnic was the best one she'd ever been to.

   She _____ a good time.
   (have)

2. Fred would have won the pie-eating contest if he had taken his sister's advice.

   He _____ to her.
   (listen)

3. We called Nancy last night, but she wasn't home.

   She _____ to a movie.
   (go)

4. Mrs. Golo can't get in the house.

   She _____ her keys.
   (lose)

5. It rained this morning, and Sam got wet while he was walking to work.

   He _____ his umbrella.
   (take)

6. Johnnie shouldn't have gotten into a fight with Barry Craxton.

   He _____ hurt.
   (get)

7. It's too bad Anne wasn't able to finish her song.

   She _____ the contest if she hadn't left the stage.
   (win)

8. Ed made a bad impression at the job interview because he wasn't dressed properly.

   He _____ a suit and tie.
   (wear)

9. Only a few people came to Victoria's party Saturday night.

   She _____ very disappointed.
   (be)

10. Linda got into trouble for staying out late.

    She _____ home earlier.
    (come)

DISCUSSION • *The following paragraphs refer to the events that took place at the Disco Club the other night, when Johnnie went to see Anne take part in the singing contest. As you may recall, that night Johnnie got into a fight with Barry Craxton, who was later thrown out of the club by the manager. What do you think about the actions of these characters? Give your own opinions.*

1. To begin with, Johnnie didn't have to go looking for Anne at the Disco Club. He could have tried to forget her. He might have gotten her off his mind by reading a book or by going to a movie. But he felt that he had to see her and went to the Disco Club.

   Do you think Johnnie did the right thing? Why or why not?
   What would you have done if you had been Johnnie?

2. There are several things Johnnie could have done when Barry threw the tomato at Anne. He could have called the manager, he could have thrown a tomato at Barry's girlfriend (that is, if he had had a tomato), or he could have left the Disco Club without doing anything. But he decided to fight Barry.

   Do you think he did the right thing? Why or why not?
   What would you have done in the same situation?

3. There are several things Barry could have done when Johnnie came up and challenged him to a fight. He could have ignored Johnnie, he could have thrown another tomato at Anne, or he could have called the manager. Instead, he just stood there and laughed at Johnnie.

   Do you think Barry did the right thing? Why or why not?
   What would you have done if you had been Barry?

4. Anne didn't have to leave the stage when Barry threw the tomato at her. She could have stayed and finished her song, she could have called the manager, or she could have picked up the tomato and thrown it back at Barry. Instead, she ran over and hit Barry with her guitar.

   Do you think Anne did the right thing? Why or why not?
   What would you have done if you had been Anne?

5. The manager didn't have to throw Barry out of the club for hitting Anne with a tomato and fighting with Johnnie. He could have said to Barry, "You throw a tomato very well." He could have told Johnnie and Barry to shake hands and be friends, or he could have ignored the situation altogether. But he knew that Barry was responsible for all the trouble and made him leave the club.

   Do you think the manager did the right thing? Why or why not?
   What would you have done if you had been the manager?

FREE RESPONSE

1. Do you have any special talents or abilities, such as singing, dancing, or playing a musical instrument?
2. Have you ever taken part in a contest? Did you win?
3. Have you ever given a party? What kind of preparations did you make?
4. When was the last time you received a compliment? What was it for?
5. Do you ever get into arguments? What do you argue about?
6. What kinds of things make you nervous or uncomfortable?
7. How do you relax?
8. How do you keep in shape? Do you get much exercise?
9. What is the best way to stay healthy?

Peter Smith had a real adventure in Zorapunga, and he enjoyed telling his friends about it. Although he had taken many trips all over the world, this was the first time he had crash-landed in the jungle, or been rescued by native tribesmen. You don't have to travel to faraway places like Zorapunga to have an exciting trip; you only need to have a spirit of adventure. Travel can be a way of living out fantasies, of turning a dream into reality.

When Peter takes a trip he usually goes on his own instead of traveling with an organized tour. He likes the freedom of deciding where he will go, what he will do when he gets there, and how long he will stay. He enjoys exploring remote areas where there are no tourists. His idea of travel is based on a desire to escape, at least temporarily, from all that is familiar. When he is in a foreign country, he is determined to participate and not to play the role of a passive observer. Perhaps that explains why Peter has had so many exciting and memorable experiences during his travels.

Along with the advantages, there are certain disadvantages in traveling alone. For inexperienced travelers, a trip can be and often is a series of minor catastrophes and disappointments: failure to understand the language, not being able to ask directions, taking the wrong bus and getting off at the wrong place, being stared at, eating unfamiliar food, and spending sleepless nights in unfamiliar quarters. Even experienced travelers can have these problems, as Peter found out when he went to Zorapunga.

Not surprisingly, there are many people who prefer to travel with organized tours. They feel the advantages outweigh the disadvantages. Group tours are often cheaper than traveling alone; they can provide their members with substantial discounts on airfares and hotel accommodations. Experienced people have planned the tour and all arrangements are taken care of in advance. There is no problem with making connections or finding a hotel. Professional tour escorts look after the needs of every member of the group. And local guides are provided to show them the sights and explain the customs of the different countries. Many travelers enjoy going on organized tours because of the opportunity they have to meet other people and make friendships that can last a lifetime.

1. How was Peter's trip to Zorapunga different from his other trips?
2. Why does Peter like to travel alone?
3. What are some advantages of traveling alone?
4. What are some of the problems that inexperienced travelers have?
5. What are some of the advantages of traveling with organized tours?
6. Would you rather travel alone or with a group? Why?
7. Would you rather visit Paris or go to a place like Zorapunga? Why?

FREE RESPONSE

1. What part of the world would you like to visit?
2. Where do you want to go on your next vacation? Why do you want to go there?
3. When you take a trip, would you rather make your own arrangements or have everything taken care of by a travel agency? Why?
4. Would you rather travel alone or with a group? Why?
5. What places do tourists like to visit in your country? Why are these places popular?
6. When was the last time you took a trip? Where did you go? What did you do there?
7. What unusual experiences have you had while traveling?
8. What do you enjoy most about traveling?
9. Have you met any interesting people while traveling?
10. Have you ever visited a place that was so wonderful it made you want to stay and live there?

ROLE PLAY

Student A plays a tourist representative for his or her country. Student B plays a traveler who wants to visit that country.

Situation: The tourist representative answers the traveler's questions about the representative's country, including interesting places to visit, the weather, transportation, food, hotels, shopping, and so on.

COMPOSITION

1. Write about your ideal vacation. What would it be like?
2. Write about an interesting place you have visited.

VOCABULARY

act (n.)
admit
adult (n.)
amateur (adj.)
amaze
anxious
appetite
athletic

bite (v.)
boo (v.)

cannibal (n.)
celebrate
challenge (v.)
chew (v.)
chin (n.)
circle (n.)
civilization
clever
combine (v.)
contact (n.)

contest (n.)
contestant

desperate
destination
destroy
determination
diet (v.)
disqualify
drum (n.)

escape (v.)
exist
exotic

faint (v.)
fist
fluent

gamble (v.)
grateful
gutter

halfway
hidden (adj.)
hunger

ignore
irritate

jungle

lodging (n.)

magic (adj.)
malt (n.)
miracle
native (n.)
negative
(adj.)

overweight

pleasure
prize (n.)

prove

race (n.)
refreshment
region
remark (v.)
reserve (v.)

sacrifice (n.)
sea
secret (adj.)
secretly
secure (adj.)
settle (v.)
steady
storm (n.)
survive

thirst (n.)
tie
tropical
tune (n.)

unbearable

village

washcloth

yard

EXPRESSIONS

to be disqualified
to be irritated
to make sure

to take part (in something)
to get away with something
to stand in line

best of all
in spite of
all by himself

Come on.
That's nothing.
Take care.

I can't figure you out.
Don't you see?
I'm in love with you.

The contest was almost over.
She couldn't spare the time.
She lost her temper.

My mind is made up.
You're so stubborn.
You don't care about me.

What do you mean?
It doesn't matter.
Let's drop the whole thing.

You aren't up to it.
I'm on your side.
You don't have the nerve.

We didn't sleep a wink.
That isn't true.
Probably not.

THIRD CONDITIONAL

He would have passed the test if he had studied.
She wouldn't have forgotten her umbrella if she hadn't been in a hurry.

PERFECT MODALS:

SHOULD HAVE

They came late and missed most of the party.	They should have come earlier.
He got sick from eating too much food.	He shouldn't have eaten so much.

COULD HAVE

She was a good student in high school.	She could have gone to college.
We didn't have to walk home yesterday.	We could have taken the bus.

MIGHT HAVE

We don't know for sure that he fed the dog.	He might have forgotten.
It's possible that they didn't go to the beach.	They might have gone to the park.

MUST HAVE

Barbara went to bed as soon as she got home.	She must have been tired.
Nick was smiling after his chess game with Fred.	He must have won the game.

Chapter 6

TOPICS
Your family history
Music
Success
Jobs

GRAMMAR
Future continuous
Future perfect
Uses of "get" (review)

FUNCTIONS
Talking about the future
Communicating without words
Making predictions
Giving opinions

SATURDAY MORNING

SUNDAY MORNING

SUNDAY NIGHT

MONDAY MORNING

COLOSSEUM

MONDAY AFTERNOON

VATICAN

1. *Talk about the pictures.*
2. *Listen to the story.*
3. *Answer the story questions.*

It's Saturday morning. Tino and Barbara Martinoli are at home looking at a map of Italy. Tino is pointing to the city of Florence, where he was born. When Tino was five years old, his family left Italy and came to live in the United States. They settled in Wickam City, where Tino's father opened an Italian restaurant.

Ever since Tino was a little boy, he has wanted to return to his birthplace and visit his relatives, who are still living in Florence. Now, at the age of twenty-nine, he has finally decided to make the trip. Tomorrow at this time Tino will be flying over the Atlantic on his way to Italy. Barbara won't be going with him because she has to stay and work at the bank. Tino will arrive at the Rome Airport about nine o'clock Sunday night. He will spend the night at the Colombo Hotel. On Monday Tino will be doing some sightseeing in Rome. He will visit the Colosseum and the Vatican, including the famous Sistine Chapel.

On Tuesday morning Tino will take the train to Florence. Some of his relatives will meet him at the train station. They don't speak English, so Tino will be speaking with them in Italian. He is a little embarrassed because his Italian is not very good. While he is in Florence, Tino will be staying with his uncle's family. They have an apartment near the Ponte Vecchio. Tino will be spending five days in Florence. He will be returning to the United States on the following Sunday. One week is a very short time to spend in Italy and Tino wishes he could stay longer, but he knows it won't be the last time he will be visiting the country where he was born.

1. Where was Tino born?
2. How old was he when his family left Italy?
3. What has Tino wanted to do ever since he was a little boy?
4. What will he be doing this time tomorrow?
5. Why won't Barbara be going with him?
6. When will Tino arrive at the Rome Airport?
7. What famous places will he visit on Monday?
8. When will Tino take the train to Florence?
9. Who will meet him at the train station?
10. What language will Tino be speaking with his relatives?
11. Why is he a little embarrassed?
12. How long will Tino be staying in Italy?

FUTURE CONTINUOUS

Tino will be flying to Italy tomorrow.

_____ staying with his uncle's family.

_____ speaking Italian with his relatives.

_____ seeing a lot of interesting things.

We use the **future continuous** to talk about actions that will be in progress at a specific time in the future.

PAIR WORK • *Ask and answer questions about the people in the pictures.*

1. Tino/now   he/on Sunday

A: **What is Tino doing now?**
B: **He's packing his suitcase.**
A: **What will he be doing on Sunday?**
B: **He'll be flying to Italy.**

2. Sam and Mabel/today   they/tomorrow

A: **What are Sam and Mabel doing today?**
B: **They're painting the house.**
A: **What will they be doing tomorrow?**
B: **They'll be resting.**

3. Jimmy and Linda/now   they/an hour from now

4. Peter/today   he/tomorrow

5. Mrs. Golo/now   she/in a little while

6. Otis and Gloria/now   they/tonight

7. Dr. Pasto/now   he/an hour from now

8. Carlos and Luisa/now   they/after dinner

Listen and practice.

Sunday morning Barbara drove Tino to the airport. When she got home she found a visitor waiting at the door. It was Johnnie Wilson.

BARBARA: Johnnie, what a surprise. I haven't seen you in ages.

JOHNNIE: Hello, Barbara. Where's Tino?

BARBARA: I just saw him off at the airport. He's flying to Italy.

JOHNNIE: Italy? Why is he going there?

BARBARA: He wants to visit his relatives in Florence. He hasn't seen them since he was a little boy.

JOHNNIE: How long will Tino be in Italy?

BARBARA: Just a week. But in a week he will have seen a lot of things.

JOHNNIE: And done a lot of traveling.

BARBARA: That's right. By the time he gets back he will have traveled over twelve thousand miles. But that's enough about Tino. How are you and Anne doing?

JOHNNIE: Terrible. She left for Hollywood last week.

BARBARA: Yes, I know. It won't be the same around here without Anne.

JOHNNIE: Oh Barbara, I feel so depressed. I'm afraid Anne won't come back to Wickam City and I'll never see her again.

BARBARA: Don't be silly. She has to come back before the election. She plans to vote for Otis.

JOHNNIE: The election is two months off. By that time she will have become a famous singer. She will have found a new boyfriend and forgotten all about me.

BARBARA: You never forget the ones who really count, Johnnie. But if Anne means so much to you, why didn't you go to Hollywood with her?

JOHNNIE: She didn't want me to go, and I didn't want to be in the way. When I tried to give her some advice, she told me to mind my own business.

BARBARA: She's got to find out some things for herself, Johnnie. In the meantime, all you can do is hope for the best.

JOHNNIE: I suppose you're right. Well, I'd better be going. See you later, Barbara.

BARBARA: Good-bye, Johnnie. And try not to worry.

FUTURE PERFECT

She will have become a famous singer by then.
_____ found a new boyfriend by then.
_____ forgotten about Johnnie by then.

We use the **future perfect** for an action that will have been completed by a certain time in the future.

PAIR WORK • *Have conversations similar to the examples.*

> A: Will Anne still be in Wickam City next week?
> B: No, she **will have left** by then. (leave)
>
> A: Will she be thinking about Johnnie a month from now?
> B: No, she **will have forgotten him** by then. (forget him)

1. A: Will Tino still be in Italy next month?
   B: No, he _____ by then. (come back)

2. A: Will the Browns be living in the same house a year from now?
   B: No, they _____ by then. (move)

3. A: Will Gloria still be working at six o'clock?
   B: No, she _____ by then. (go home)

4. A: Will Sam still be cleaning the garage tomorrow?
   B: No, he _____ by then. (finish)

5. A: Will Jack be driving the same car a year from now?
   B: No, he _____ by then. (sell it)

6. A: Will Nancy be using our camera after this Sunday?
   B: No, she _____ by then. (return it)

7. A: Will Maria be sleeping at eight in the morning?
   B: No, she _____ by then. (get up)

8. A: Will Mr. Bascomb still be working ten years from now?
   B: No, he _____ by then. (retire)

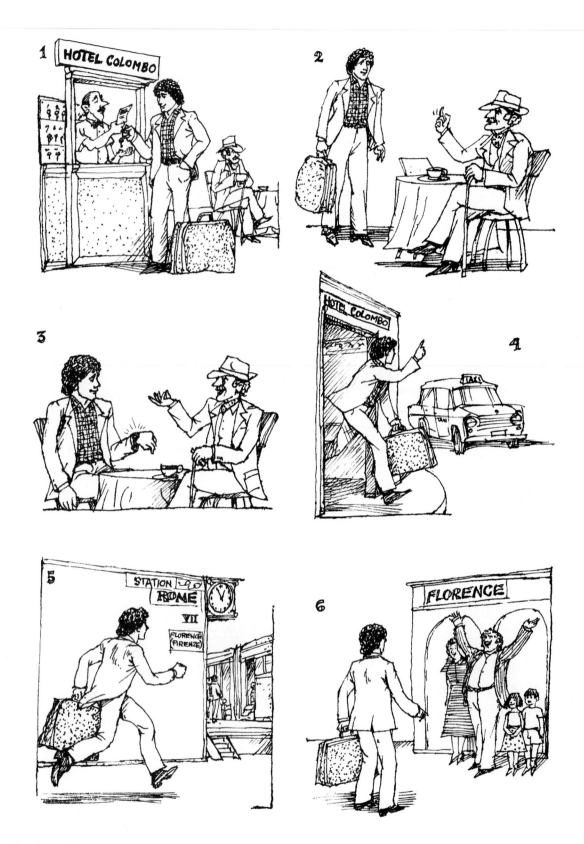

1. Talk about the pictures.
2. Listen to the story.
3. Answer the story questions.

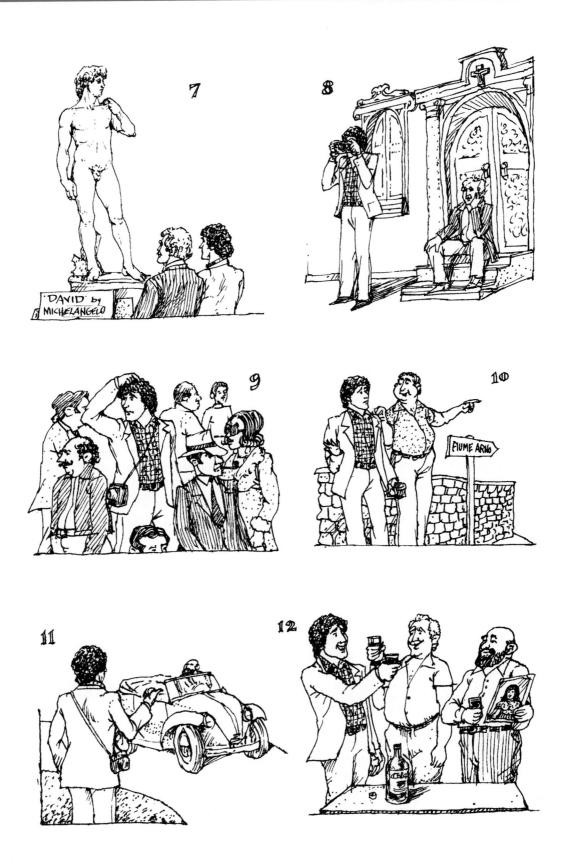

READING

Before Tino went to the airport last Sunday, Suzi Suzuki asked him to write a letter describing his trip to Italy. She wanted to have it published in the travel section of the Wickam Daily News. *Tino sent the letter from Florence on Wednesday.*

Wednesday

Dear Suzi,

I've finally got some time to write the letter I promised for the *Daily News*. This is only my third day in Italy and already I've had some very interesting experiences. On Monday morning I visited the Colosseum, where Christians were thrown to the lions almost two thousand years ago. As I stood in the center of the Colosseum, I imagined how frightened the Christians must have been as they faced the lions. On Monday afternoon I went to the Vatican and saw the Sistine Chapel, with its famous paintings by Michelangelo. The figures he painted on the ceiling of the chapel are so beautiful they can't be described. I got some photographs of the Vatican and the Colosseum, which I'll show you all when I get back to Wickam City.

On Tuesday morning I almost missed the train to Florence. I was about to leave the hotel when I got into a conversation with a wealthy Italian gentleman. He said that he had lived in the United States many years ago. In spite of his wealth, he seemed to be a very unhappy man. I guess he was just lonely and didn't have anyone to talk to. He started telling me all about his younger days in America. I finally had to excuse myself and hurry out of the hotel. When I got outside, I called a taxi and rushed to the train station. I managed to get there just in time to take the train.

When I got to Florence, my relatives were there to meet me at the train station. You can't imagine what it was like seeing them again after all these years. I got so excited I could hardly talk. You know my Italian isn't very good, but somehow we managed to communicate all right. My uncle Giovanni kept saying, *"Benvenuto in Italia, Tino, benvenuto in Italia,"* which means "Welcome to Italy." We had lunch in a little cafe and then went to Giovanni's apartment, which has a nice view of the Ponte Vecchio.

The weather in Florence is very pleasant at this time of year. It's sunny and warm during the day but gets cool after dark. It's a good thing I brought my wool sweater to wear in the evening.

The ladies would really enjoy shopping in Florence. They make so many beautiful things here. I mustn't forget to get Barbara something before I leave!

This morning Giovanni took me to see the statue of *David.* It's really an incredible work of art. You never get tired of looking at it. We stayed there for a while and then drove to the Piazza della Signoria. When we got there, I felt like walking around and taking pictures. There were so many interesting things to see. But Giovanni was tired and needed a rest. He said he would wait for me in front of an old church near the square. You won't believe what happened then! I got so carried away taking pictures that I didn't pay attention to where I was going and got lost. I didn't remember the name of the church Giovanni mentioned and couldn't find my way back. Finally, I got someone to point to where the river was, and I started walking in that direction.

When I got to the river, I could see the Ponte Vecchio in the distance. It was at least two miles away. I didn't feel like walking any more so I started hitchhiking. I was lucky and got a ride after waiting only a few minutes. Now, wait until you hear this! The man who picked me up is an old friend of my uncle's. His name is Frederico. When I told him who I was, he insisted on taking me all the way to Giovanni's apartment. Giovanni was there when we arrived. You can imagine how glad he was to see us. But when he found out that I had hitchhiked, he warned me not to do it again. He thanked Frederico for bringing me home safely.

Frederico was in excellent spirits. He told us his daughter was getting married at the end of the month. And he invited me to go the wedding as his special guest. I was very flattered but couldn't accept his invitation. It would have meant extending my trip at least ten days, and I didn't want to be away from home that long. It's been wonderful getting to know my relatives after all this time, but I'm anxious to get back to Wickam City. It'll be good to see you all again.

Yours,

Tino

1. What famous places did Tino visit while he was in Rome?
2. What happened as Tino was about to leave the hotel Tuesday morning?
3. What did the old gentleman talk about?
4. Why was Tino in a hurry?
5. Who met him when he arrived in Florence?
6. Where did Tino stay while he was in Florence?
7. What famous statue did Tino see Wednesday morning?
8. What happened to Tino at the Piazza della Signoria?
9. How did Tino get back to Giovanni's apartment?
10. Why couldn't Tino accept Frederico's invitation to his daughter's wedding?

FREE RESPONSE

1. Have you ever gotten lost?
2. Where is the best place to go for help when you're lost?
3. What is the best way to avoid getting lost?
4. Do you think you could get around in a foreign country if you didn't know the language? How would you communicate?
5. Have you ever helped a tourist in your city?
6. What are some cities or countries where people are very friendly to tourists?
7. Do you know any places where the people are not friendly?

PRACTICE • *Make equivalent sentences using the verb* **get.**

> Tino arrived at the station just in time to take the train.
> **Tino got to the station just in time to get the train.**

1. You must convince Mrs. Grove to see a doctor.
2. Her condition is becoming worse every day.
3. Her son has just gone to pick up some medicine at the drugstore.
4. We asked him to buy some magazines for his mother.
5. I tried to reach the doctor on the phone a little while ago.
6. He won't arrive at the office until noon.
7. Mrs. Grove received a letter from her brother, "Lemon," this morning.
8. I don't know how he ever acquired the nickname "Lemon."

WRITTEN EXERCISE • *Complete the sentences using the most appropriate expressions from the list below. Each expression may be used only once.*

get bored	get hired	get married	get tired
get excited	get hurt	get paid	get upset
get fired	get lost	get scared	get wet

> Tino *got lost* because he didn't pay attention to where he was going.
> Alberta *got excited* when she won first prize in the singing contest.

1. Ms. Fern _____ because she was the best person for the job.

2. Mr. Farley _____ because he was always late to work.

3. Sam _____ because he worked all day without taking a rest.

4. Barbara _____ extra for working overtime last Friday.

5. Fred _____ because he didn't have anything to do.

6. Gloria _____ when she saw a strange man following her.

7. I'm glad no one _____ in the automobile accident yesterday.

8. Johnnie _____ when he went out in the rain without his umbrella.

9. Gladys _____ when the waiter spilled soup on her dress.

10. Candy and Rico _____ last month. I went to their wedding.

Listen and practice.

BARBARA: Welcome back, darling. I missed you.

TINO: I missed you too, Barbara. It's good to be home.

BARBARA: I got the postcards you sent. It sounds like you had a good time in Italy.

TINO: I had a great time. Everything went beautifully.

BARBARA: What was the best part of your trip?

TINO: Being with my relatives. They're really wonderful people. It's too bad you couldn't go with me, Barbara. You would have enjoyed meeting Giovanni and his family.

BARBARA: I know, it would have been fun, even though I can't speak Italian.

TINO: You can communicate a lot of things without words, Barbara. And that reminds me, here's a picture taken the day I arrived in Florence. You can see me with my relatives in front of their apartment.

BARBARA: It's a nice photograph, Tino. Everyone looks so happy. Who's the old woman next to you?

TINO: That's my grandmother, Eleanora. She's eighty-four years old and she's incredible. You wouldn't believe how active she is in spite of her age.

BARBARA:	I'll bet she's a good cook. You look as if you've gained a few pounds.
TINO:	You're right. She's a wonderful cook, and a good storyteller too. She told me quite a bit about the history of the Martinoli family.
BARBARA:	It must have been very interesting. You're lucky you got to learn more about your family.
TINO:	It's something I've always wanted to do, Barbara. I think it's important to know your roots.
BARBARA:	You must be very proud of being Italian, Tino.
TINO:	Of course, but on this trip I also learned how American I am.
BARBARA:	That's good, because we're having hamburgers and French fries for dinner tonight.

TALKING ABOUT YOUR FAMILY HISTORY

Tino has always been very proud of his Italian ancestry. He was glad when he had the opportunity to go back to Florence and visit his relatives. By tracing his roots, he was able to learn a great deal about himself and his family.

1. Where were you born?
2. Where do your ancestors come from?
3. What language is spoken in your family?
4. Are there any good storytellers in your family?
5. What have you learned from your older relatives about your family's history?
6. Do you think it's important for people to trace their roots? Why?
7. Is there any special food or music that people in your family enjoy?
8. What is there about your family that makes you proud?

GROUP WORK • *Discuss these questions.*

- Do people always say what they are thinking and feeling?
- How can people communicate without words?
- What are some common gestures people use to communicate?
- What are some attitudes that we express through facial expressions and body language?

"Hello, Anne, please come in. I got a call from Pinky yesterday telling me all about you, and I've already made some arrangements." The speaker was Mr. Goodbar, the Hollywood agent whose address Dr. Pasto had given Anne in Wickam City. She had taken the bus the night before and was now in Hollywood, but for the life of her, she couldn't figure out who Pinky was.

"Pinky?" she said. "Do you mean Dr. Pasto?"

"Yes, Pinky Pasto," explained Mr. Goodbar. "Don't tell me Pinky never told you about our tap dancing team. We were known as the 'Four Fastest Feet in Show Business.' I guess that was before your time, my dear. I called him Pinky because he always wore a pink carnation in his buttonhole. Pinky was quite a ladies' man, too. Did he ever tell you about the time we took a dozen showgirls out for a champagne breakfast?"

"No, I don't think he ever mentioned that," said Anne. She found it difficult to imagine quiet, dignified Dr. Pasto the way Mr. Goodbar was describing him.

"Now, Anne," Mr. Goodbar went on, "we've got to work fast. I've arranged a room for you at a small hotel near here, and I've set up a busy schedule for you. At ten tomorrow you rehearse your act at the Rainbow Studio. At twelve you have lunch with the director and me, and at two o'clock you have an audition. I've also arranged for you to sing in a small nightclub on Hollywood Boulevard, and you'll be appearing on a local TV program on Saturday. I know it's a heavy schedule, but it's necessary for you to get all the exposure you can as quickly as possible."

"My, that certainly is a heavy schedule," said Anne. "At least I'll be able to relax at night."

"Oh no, Anne," said Mr. Goodbar. "You'll be going to parties every night. That's the most important part. I've arranged it so that you'll be asked to sing, and there's always the chance that someone important might see you. All important business in Hollywood gets done at parties, you know."

"But Mr. Goodbar," said Anne. "I won't have any time to myself. My life won't be my own."

"That's what it means to be a star," said Mr. Goodbar gently. "From now on you belong to me, the studios, and the public. We're going to give you new clothes, a new hairstyle, and a new name. You'll be a completely different person. Even your friends from Wickam City won't be able to recognize you."

"But Mr. Goodbar," protested Anne, "I'm not sure I . . ."

"Don't worry, Anne, you don't have to thank me. I enjoy helping people, and any friend of Pinky's is a friend of mine. Just think, soon you'll be known as Annie Angel, the girl with the sweetest voice this side of heaven."

Mr. Goodbar was an excellent agent, with many contacts, and everything happened just the way he said it would. Before she knew it, Anne was living the life of a Hollywood celebrity. All of her time was taken up by parties, TV shows, nightclub performances, interviews, and auditions. In the beginning she loved it, it was all so new and exciting. At the very first party she met an aspiring actor, Stirling Strongjaw, who became her regular escort. He was tall, muscular, and very handsome, with wavy blond hair, deep blue eyes, and a perfect tan. He was a wonderful dancer, and Anne loved the romantic way he looked deep into her eyes.

After a while, though, she got tired of the constant activities and all the clever, sophisticated people who never seemed to have anything serious to say. She began to notice little things about Stirling, such as the way he always looked at himself in the mirror, and the fact that he never stopped combing his hair. She realized that she had never had a serious conversation with him. As a matter of fact, the only thing he liked to talk about was himself. Anne began to miss her old friends from Wickam City and the long talks she used to have with Johnnie. Finally, the night before she was to sign the contract for a national singing tour, the contract she had dreamed about, she decided to have a serious talk with Stirling.

"Stirling," she said. "Stop doing your exercises a minute and come here, please. I'd like to talk with you."

"An actor has to keep in shape, my love," he said. "Besides, what is there to talk about?"

"That's just it, Stirling, what do you like to talk about?" said Anne. "Haven't you read any interesting books lately?"

"I don't like to read much," said Stirling, flexing his muscles, "but did you see the reviews I got in the latest issue of *Show Business Magazine?*"

"No, I didn't. But listen, Stirling, what would you say if I told you I had decided not to sign that contract tomorrow?"

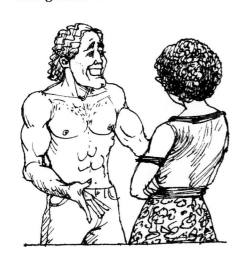

"You what?" exclaimed Stirling, shocked. "But you can't do that, Anne, it's our big chance. I mean, it's your big chance. Can't you see it, when we're . . . I mean when you're on the cover of *Stage and Screen Magazine,* it'll be great publicity for me—I mean for you. . . ."

"But Stirling," said Anne, "if I go on tour we won't be together any more. We'll never see each other. What kind of life is that?"

"But Anne, I've already gotten offers for movie parts just because I'm your boyfriend. Everyone knows you'll be appearing on national television. By this time next year, you'll have been all over the country on tour. You'll be famous. Please, Anne, don't throw away this big chance. Don't let me down."

"That's just what I thought, Stirling. You aren't really interested in me at all. You're only interested in my fame and what it can do for your career."

"But Anne, that's show business. And don't you want to prove that you can be a success?"

Anne didn't say anything. She walked across the room and looked out the window. She thought about Wickam City and all the friends she had left behind. They were good friends, and they were always there when she needed them, especially Johnnie. Then she turned around and looked at Stirling, who was looking at himself in the mirror again.

"I've already proved that I'm a success," she said. "I've proved it to myself, and that's what really counts. Now all I want is for you to get out of here and leave me alone. I'm going back to the people who really care about me, who like me for what I am and not for what I can do for them—real people who have more going for them than nice hair and big muscles. Good-bye, Stirling, and good-bye Hollywood."

STORY QUESTIONS

1. Who is Mr. Goodbar?
2. How did he help Anne?
3. Why was it important for her to go to parties?
4. Who did Anne meet at the first party she went to?
5. What did Anne like about Stirling?
6. What is your opinion of Stirling?
7. What was the real reason Stirling wanted Anne to become a famous singer?
8. Why did Anne decide to go back to Wickam City?
9. What did Anne learn from her experience in Hollywood?
10. Do you think it's possible for a person to be too ambitious?

PRACTICE • *Make predictions about Anne, Stirling, and yourself. What do you think the three of you will have done or won't have done by this time next year?*

> **I think Anne will have gotten married.**
> OR **I don't think Anne will have gotten married.**

Anne

1. get married
2. buy a house
3. become a parent
4. start her own business

Stirling

1. find a new girlfriend
2. get married
3. become a famous actor
4. travel around the world

You

1. become fluent in English
2. move to another city
3. fall in love
4. get rich

PAIR WORK • *Ask and answer questions using **will be doing** or **might be doing**.*

> five minutes after this class is over
> A: **What do you think you'll be doing five minutes after this class is over?**
> B: **I'll (probably) be walking home.** OR **I might be having a cup of coffee.**

1. five minutes after this class is over
2. at 10:30 tonight
3. tomorrow morning at 7:30
4. next Saturday at noon
5. at this time next week
6. a year from now

FREE RESPONSE

1. Where do you think you'll be living by the end of this year?
2. What do you think you'll be doing five years from now?
3. Do you think you'll be living better? How?
4. What are two things you think you'll have done by the end of this year?
5. Do you think you'll have become rich or famous by the end of your life?

PRACTICE • *Change the sentences using **get** + the passive form of the verb.*

Someone <u>lost</u> the keys.	They <u>delayed</u> the meeting for an hour.
The keys got lost.	**The meeting got delayed for an hour.**

1. Someone <u>broke</u> the gate yesterday.
2. They <u>criticized</u> Fred for being lazy.
3. Something <u>scared</u> the cat and it wouldn't go outside.
4. A police officer <u>stopped</u> Jack for driving too fast.
5. They <u>canceled</u> the meeting at the last minute.
6. The company <u>paid</u> all the workers.
7. Someone <u>stole</u> my bicycle.
8. They <u>delivered</u> the package to the wrong address.
9. Someone <u>threw out</u> the old magazines.
10. They <u>did</u> all the housework in three hours.

WRITTEN EXERCISE • *Make original sentences using the following expressions with **get**.*

get mad *My sister got mad when I broke the mirror.*

get better *Tino's Italian is getting better.*

1. get home _____
2. get lost _____
3. get tired _____
4. get depressed _____
5. get worse _____
6. get sick _____
7. get rich _____
8. get married _____
9. get nervous _____
10. get better _____

FREE RESPONSE

1. When was the last time you got mad? What happened?
2. Have you ever gotten criticized unfairly? What for?
3. What would you do if you got bad service in a restaurant?
4. How do you get people to do what you want?
5. How long does it take you to get ready for a special occasion?
6. What do you think is the best age to get married?
7. How do people change as they get older?
8. What are some advantages of getting older?
9. How is your life getting better?
10. Why is it important to get a good education?

WRITTEN EXERCISE • *Complete the conditional sentences using the correct form of the verbs in parentheses.*

If you take my advice, you ___*will pay*___ more attention to your health.
(pay)

You ___*would feel*___ better if you got more exercise.
(feel)

I ___*would have played*___ tennis yesterday if I hadn't been so busy.
(play)

1. I wish I _____ a car, so I wouldn't have to take a bus.
   (have)

2. If I had enough money, I _____ a car.
   (buy)

3. If you lived closer to your job, you _____ to work.
   (walk)

4. If you _____ harder, you would be more successful.
   (work)

5. We'll have a picnic this Saturday if the weather _____ good.
   (be)

6. Peter doesn't plan to come, but if he changes his mind, he _____ us.
   (tell)

7. If you had come to the party last week, you _____ a good time.
   (have)

8. If I _____ you, I would go out more often.
   (be)

9. If I _____ you were home yesterday, I would have called you.
   (know)

FREE RESPONSE

1. What will you do if the weather is good on Saturday?
2. How will you feel if it rains tomorrow?
3. What will happen to you if you eat too much candy?
4. Where would you live if you could live anywhere in the world?
5. What languages do you wish you could speak?
6. If you could have any job, what would you like to do?
7. What would you do if you had more free time?
8. How do you think your life would have been different if you'd been born in the United States?
9. How would you have reacted if the president had invited you for dinner last week?
10. Would you have been happier if you'd lived another time in history?

ROLE PLAY • *Choose one of these situations and make up a conversation. Role play the conversation before the class.*

Contemporary American music is as varied as American society. The tastes, attitudes, values, and lifestyle of a people are reflected in the music of that society. Some say that music is the heart and soul of a culture. A simple melody will often produce feelings or moods that few other art forms are able to match. With these points in mind, let us look at the three most popular types of American music: country, jazz, and rock.

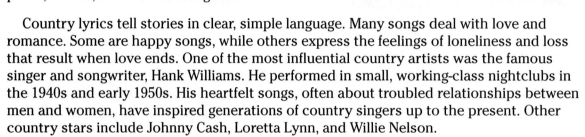

Country music developed in the southern region of the United States during the 1800s. It combined elements of folk music from Britain, the blues of southern Blacks, and southern religious music. The basic instruments in early country bands were the fiddle, the banjo, and the guitar. Over the decades, country musicians have added other instruments, including the piano, drums, and the electric guitar.

Country lyrics tell stories in clear, simple language. Many songs deal with love and romance. Some are happy songs, while others express the feelings of loneliness and loss that result when love ends. One of the most influential country artists was the famous singer and songwriter, Hank Williams. He performed in small, working-class nightclubs in the 1940s and early 1950s. His heartfelt songs, often about troubled relationships between men and women, have inspired generations of country singers up to the present. Other country stars include Johnny Cash, Loretta Lynn, and Willie Nelson.

Jazz has often been called the greatest American art form. The music grew from a combination of influences, including the blues, African rhythms, and American band traditions and instruments. The earliest jazz was performed by Black musicians in the late 1800s who had little or no formal training in music. As jazz grew in popularity, its sound was influenced by musicians with formal training and classical backgrounds.

Jazz may be performed by a single musician, by a small group of musicians called a *combo,* or by a *big band* of ten or more pieces. A traditional jazz band consists of a *front line* of a trumpet, trombone, and a clarinet or saxophone, and a *rhythm section* of drums, a bass, a piano, and often a guitar or banjo. The front line instruments perform the melodies and most of the solos. The rhythm section maintains the steady beat and adds interesting rhythm patterns.

One of the key elements of jazz is improvisation: the ability to create new music spontaneously. Improvisation raises the role of the soloist from just a performer of others' ideas to a composer as well. And it gives jazz a fresh excitement at each performance.

Fully developed jazz probably originated in New Orleans at the beginning of the 1900s. New Orleans–style jazz emerged from the city's own musical traditions of band music for funeral processions and street parades. Today, this type of jazz is called traditional jazz or Dixieland jazz. Not surprisingly, New Orleans was the musical home of the first notable players and composers of jazz, including trumpeter Louis Armstrong and pianist Jelly Roll Morton.

Dixieland jazz was followed in the 1930s by a more sophisticated type of jazz called swing. During the swing era, people danced to the big band music of Duke Ellington, Benny Goodman, Glenn Miller, and Count Basie. Dixieland and swing have maintained their popularity over the years as newer jazz forms have come along, including bebop, cool jazz, and fusion. Jazz in all its forms has gained international popularity, with American jazz bands performing for enthusiastic audiences overseas.

Rock music is one of the world's most popular musical forms. When it originated in the United States in the 1950s, rock music was known as "rock'n'roll." From the start it was party music, dance music, and music that appealed to young listeners. It often expressed the joys of being young, and it occasionally expressed the frustrations of youth.

Rock grew out of black rhythm and blues and white country music. Both of these musical forms are traditions in the southern state of Mississippi, the birthplace of Elvis Presley, "The King" of rock'n'roll. Although he was white, he had the style commonly associated with popular black music. His exciting live performances and frequent radio play quickly made Presley a superstar. And the rock'n'roll explosion began.

In the 1960s rock groups from England burst onto the scene. The Beatles and the Rolling Stones turned rock'n'roll into an international phenomenon. Their lifestyles became models for young people to follow. The rock musicians grew their hair long and wore beads and brightly colored clothing, and so did their followers. Another important force was Bob Dylan, who influenced the 60s generation with his "protest songs." These songs cried out against what many people considered the wrongs of society, such as racial prejudice, poverty, and war.

Throughout the 1970s, almost all popular music contained elements of the rock style. As the audiences for rock grew, a variety of new musical categories developed, such as *country rock* and *jazz rock.* During the 1980s and 1990s, several rock artists incorporated the music of Africa and Latin America into their music. It is the ability of rock music to adapt, innovate, and create new sounds and lyrics that accounts for much of rock's success.

As we have seen, rock, jazz, and country music have much in common. They all originated in the South and have borrowed heavily from one another. They express life with all its joys, struggles, and heartaches. In the words of the immortal Ray Charles, "They stir up your insides and make you *feel* something."

1. What were the basic instruments in early country music?
2. Why do many country songs make you feel sad?
3. What types of music influenced the early sound of jazz?
4. What is improvisation?
5. Why is New Orleans important in the history of jazz?
6. What is the best jazz style for dancing?
7. What are the roots of rock music?
8. Why does rock music appeal to young people?
9. Why was Elvis Presley called "The King" of rock'n'roll?
10. Who were the Beatles? How did they affect rock music?
11. What do rock, jazz, and country music have in common?

ONE STEP FURTHER

TALKING ABOUT MUSIC

1. Is music your favorite kind of entertainment?
2. What kind of music do you like?
3. Who are your favorite musicians?
4. How do you feel about rock music? Have you ever been to a rock concert?
5. Do you think rock music will be as popular in the future as it is now?
6. How popular is rock music in your country? What about jazz?
7. What other kinds of music are popular in your country?
8. What kind of music is best for dancing?
9. Is there a special place where you like to go and dance or listen to music?

TALKING ABOUT SUCCESS

Anne went to Hollywood to prove that she could be a successful singer. While she was there, she learned that having a successful career isn't everything.

1. Do you think there are some things in life that are more important than a successful career?
2. What are some qualities that successful people usually have?
3. What does it mean to be successful? How is success measured in today's society?
4. Do you think a person must be successful in business in order to be happy in life?
5. Do you think everyone can be a success? Why or why not?
6. Do you know anyone who was once a failure and later became a success? How did it happen?
7. What is your idea of success?
8. What is your idea of a happy life?
9. What do you think is the most important thing in life?

TALKING ABOUT GETTING JOBS

Dr. Pasto was able to help Anne get a start in Hollywood because he knows a lot of influential people in show business. In other words, he has "connections."

1. How important is it to have connections?
2. Do you know any people who got jobs they didn't deserve just because they had connections?
3. Have you ever lost a job or promotion you should have had?
4. Do you think a person's ability to do the job should be the only consideration?
5. How important is a person's appearance and personality in getting a job or promotion?
6. Do you think it's possible for most people to improve their appearance and personality?
7. If you were an employer, what kind of person would you want to hire?
8. Would you hire a friend even if he or she wasn't the best person for the job?

COMPOSITION

1. Write about your family history. What is unique about your family?
2. Write about the kind of music you like. Why is it meaningful to you?
3. Write about success and happiness. How do you think they can best be achieved?

VOCABULARY

acquire	darling	imagine	popularity	wavy
active	dignified (adj.)	insist	protest (v.)	wealthy
ancestor			publish	
arrangement	extend	lonely		
			relative (n.)	
beautifully	fame	muscle (n.)	review (n.)	
birthplace	figure (n.)	muscular		
body language			schedule (n.)	
	gain (v.)	national	section (n.)	
carnation	gesture (n.)	nickname (n.)	shock (v.)	
celebrity	grandmother	nightclub	somehow	
comb (v.)			sophisticated	
communicate	hairstyle	overtime	studio	
contract (n.)	heaven			
cool	hitchhike (v.)	pink (adj.)	train (n.)	

EXPRESSIONS

to throw away	to pay attention	My!
to get lost	to be in the way	just in time
to get carried away	to keep in shape	after dark
to see someone off		quite a bit

Before she knew it . . .   Leave me alone.
Her time was taken up . . .   Mind your own business.
He was a ladies' man.   Don't let me down.
That was before your time.   Don't be silly.

It's important to know your roots.   I haven't seen you in ages.
The election is two months off.   This is our big chance.
They have a lot going for them.   He was in excellent spirits.
For the life of her . . .   Any friend of his is a friend of mine.

FUTURE CONTINUOUS

They will be having a meeting this time tomorrow.
She will be studying at the library after lunch.

FUTURE PERFECT

We will have waited over an hour by the time she gets here.
They will have completed their studies by next summer.

Chapter
7

T O P I C S

Politics

Current issues

Health

Love, faith, and miracles

G R A M M A R

Participles

F U N C T I O N S

Describing a series of actions

Making complaints

Summarizing conversations

Asking for and giving information

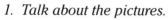

1. *Talk about the pictures.*
2. *Listen to the story.*
3. *Answer the story questions.*

Johnnie hasn't been himself lately. He used to run the best bookshop in Wickam City and had a well-deserved reputation for being courteous and efficient. He would do anything to please the people who came into his bookshop. But ever since Anne went to Hollywood, he seems to have lost interest in his work, often ignoring his customers. They have been complaining more and more about the poor service and the inefficiency at Johnnie's Bookstore.

Today has been another one of those tiring, frustrating days for Johnnie. All afternoon he has had to put up with complaints from dissatisfied customers. A few minutes before closing time his assistant, Abigail, came over to talk to him. Noticing the tired expression on Johnnie's face and feeling concerned about him, she suggested that he take a nice relaxing walk in the park. Nodding his head slowly, he agreed that it was a good idea.

As Johnnie walked through the park he heard the sounds of laughing children. He saw Marty and some other boys playing baseball. And there was Fred, giving them encouragement. They all seemed to be having so much fun, which just made Johnnie feel worse. Reaching the north end of the park, he stopped at the old wishing well. In the good old days, Johnnie remembered sadly, he and Anne had often come to the well. It was their favorite meeting place. Sitting by the well and looking at their reflections in the water, they spent many wonderful hours just talking. Now that Anne was gone, every day seemed the same, without end and without meaning. And everywhere Johnnie went there was something to remind him of the happy times he had spent with Anne. He had never thought it possible to miss someone so much. The trouble was, whenever he tried to tell Anne his true feelings he got so nervous that he could hardly talk. If only she would come home! If only he could talk to her once more.

At that very moment Anne was arriving at the bus station in Wickam City, only a short distance from City Park. She had just returned from Hollywood and was very tired, having sat on the bus for nine hours. She wanted to see Johnnie again but was afraid to approach him, not knowing what his reaction would be. After all that had happened, he might have changed his mind about her. Anne needed to relax and think about the future. Hoping to find some peace and quiet, she decided to take a walk in the park.

It was a nice sunny day and the park was beautiful, as always, but Anne was troubled. What did the future hold for her, she wondered? After her experience in Hollywood she knew that she loved Johnnie, but how did he feel about her? Did he still love her? Would he take her back? These were the thoughts that were passing through Anne's mind when suddenly she looked up and saw a familiar figure in the distance. Dropping her suitcase and guitar, she started running toward the north end of the park.

Johnnie was leaning over the edge of the well. Taking a penny from his pocket, he closed his eyes and made a wish. He wished that Anne would come back to Wickam City. Then he threw the penny into the well. When he opened his eyes again he saw Anne's face in the water. He blinked hard. He couldn't believe it was really Anne. He thought he was dreaming. Then he heard Anne's voice. Turning around slowly, he saw her standing right behind him. Johnnie was so surprised that he lost his balance and started falling backward. Anne tried to grab him but it was too late; Johnnie had fallen into the well. When she looked down, she saw that he wasn't moving, and she had a horrible, sick feeling. Not knowing how to swim, she couldn't pull Johnnie out of the water, so she started calling for help. Immediately, Fred and Marty came running over to the well. When they saw what had happened, they dove in and pulled Johnnie out of the water. He wasn't badly hurt, but he had a nasty bump on his head from the fall. Anne was so thankful he was OK that she started crying.

1. How has Johnnie's life changed since Anne went to Hollywood?
2. How have things gone for Johnnie at the bookshop today?
3. Why did Abigail suggest that Johnnie take a walk in the park?
4. What did Johnnie do when he reached the north end of the park?
5. What was special about the old wishing well?
6. Why couldn't Johnnie tell Anne his true feelings?
7. What was Anne doing that same afternoon?
8. Why was she afraid to talk to Johnnie?
9. Where did she go?
10. What did she do when she saw Johnnie?
11. Why did Johnnie take a penny from his pocket?
12. What did he wish?
13. What did he see when he opened his eyes?
14. What happened when he turned around and saw Anne standing behind him?
15. Why didn't Anne pull Johnnie out of the water?
16. What did she do?
17. What happened at the end?

PRACTICE • *Change the sentences as indicated.*

> He walked through the park and heard the sounds of laughing children.
> **Walking through the park, he heard the sounds of laughing children.**
>
> He reached the north end of the park and stopped at the old wishing well.
> **Reaching the north end of the park, he stopped at the old wishing well.**

1. He thought about Anne and felt very sad.
2. He took a penny from his pocket and made a wish.
3. He opened his eyes and saw Anne's face in the water.
4. He turned around and saw her standing behind him.
5. He lost his balance and fell into the well.
6. She felt scared and called for help.
7. They heard her voice and ran over to the well.
8. They saw what had happened and pulled Johnnie out of the water.

Listen and practice.

MARTY: He's got a big bump on his head. Do you think he's all right, Fred?

FRED: Listen, he's trying to say something.

ANNE: Johnnie, speak to me. Please speak to me!

JOHNNIE: Are you an angel from heaven?

ANNE: No, I'm Anne from Wickam.

JOHNNIE: Anne, is that really you? Or am I just dreaming?

ANNE: Yes, Johnnie, it's me. I've come back, and I'm here to stay.

JOHNNIE: Do you believe in miracles, Anne? I made a wish that you would come back, and here you are!

ANNE: Yes, I do believe in miracles, Johnnie. It's a miracle that you're all right, and that we're together again.

JOHNNIE: I love you, Anne. Please say you love me too.

MARTY: Gee, Fred, he's out of his mind!

ANNE: Shut up, Marty! Of course I love you, Johnnie. Going to Hollywood taught me a lesson. A singing career is important to me, but you're even more important. Without you, nothing has any meaning.

JOHNNIE: It's not a matter of choosing between a career and marriage, Anne. Married women have careers too. And these last few weeks have shown me that being with you is what really counts.

ANNE: Marriage? Did you say marriage? Does that mean . . . ?

FRED: He's delirious. Let's throw a bucket of water on him to bring him 'round.

ANNE: Mind your own business, Fred. He knows what he's saying.

JOHNNIE: Yes, Anne. I'm asking you to marry me. Please say yes, Anne.

ANNE: Of course I say yes, Johnnie. And Fred, Marty, would you two please leave? I'd like to be alone with my future husband.

MARTY: We'd better get a doctor, huh, Fred?

FRED: No, Marty, it's much more serious than that. We'd better get a preacher. Ha, ha, ha!

MARTY: Why are you laughing, Fred?

FRED: I can't help it. All my life, the two things I've tried hardest to avoid are marriage and a career. Now Anne and Johnnie are going to have both.

MARTY: What's so funny about that?

FRED: Nothing, really. It's just the way these things come about.

MARTY: Must be a miracle, huh, Fred?

FRED: I guess so, Marty.

WRITTEN EXERCISE 1 • *Complete the sentences using present participles as adjectives.*

> Your sister bores me. You have a ___*boring*___ sister.
> Her letter accused the man of stealing. She wrote an ___*accusing*___ letter.

1. Her arguments won't convince anyone. She doesn't have any _____ arguments.

2. Her voice frightens people. She has a _____ voice.

3. Your idea doesn't interest me. It's not a very _____ idea.

4. Mr. Bascomb's speech disappointed everyone. It was a very _____ speech.

5. His job would frustrate most people. He has a _____ job.

6. Our football team lost another game today. It's too bad we have a _____ team this year.

7. Most of the fans booed when they left the field. There were hundreds of _____ fans.

8. I'm going to relax this afternoon. My plan is to spend a _____ afternoon.

9. At Joe's Cafe the waiters sing for the customers. They're _____ waiters.

10. His story amused the kids. He told an _____ story.

11. It's wonderful to see children laugh. I love to see _____ children.

12. It's almost time to close the restaurant. _____ time is in five minutes.

WRITTEN EXERCISE 2 • *Practice making sentences with participial adjectives using the words below.*

> convincing explanation *The woman gave us a convincing explanation.*
> changing world *We live in a changing world.*
> irritating personality *That boy has an irritating personality.*

1. boring job _____

2. charming personality _____

3. confusing directions _____

4. depressing story _____

5. embarrassing situation _____

6. exciting movie _____

7. fascinating woman _____

8. interesting idea _____

9. shocking crime _____

1. Talk about the picture.
 2. Listen to the story.
3. Answer the story questions.

Campaign fever has hit Wickam City. Everyone in town has been talking about the race for mayor between Otis and Mr. Bascomb. With only a week remaining before election day, both candidates are going all out to win votes and get elected. Mr. Bascomb has been very effective in getting his message across to the people, having spent huge sums of money on television commercials and newspaper advertisements. Otis, being short of funds, has had to run a different kind of campaign. He has tried to reach as many voters as possible by holding public meetings where average citizens can speak out on the issues.

This afternoon Otis held his last scheduled meeting of the campaign, and it was standing room only. Many people in the audience stood up to speak, expressing viewpoints on a wide variety of issues. Bart Johnson, president of the Wickam Chamber of Commerce, felt that the city government should do more to encourage tourism. He said that Wickam City was losing a lot of tourist business because the town's only first-class hotel, the Wickam Hotel, was in terrible condition. The rooms had torn curtains, damaged furniture, and broken doorknobs, and there was even a cracked mirror in the dining hall. He felt the city should finance some badly needed improvements in the Wickam Hotel.

Mabel Brown was concerned about the rising cost of living. She said they would all be in trouble if they didn't stop inflation. Dr. Watkins, an unemployed university professor, claimed that unemployment had gone up 30 percent in less than a year. He said that many public employees, including teachers, police officers, and firefighters, were out of work. He felt the city had an obligation to help these people. Gloria Cole felt the city should do more to help working mothers. She said they needed a day care center where they could leave their children while they were at work. Olive Grove brought up the problem of juvenile delinquency. She claimed that she had been robbed the week before by two members of a gang. They had grabbed her purse while she was walking home. Having lived peacefully in the same neighborhood for thirty years, she was very disturbed by the recent rise in juvenile crime.

Other members of the audience talked about taxes, medical care, and education. Otis agreed that these were all matters for serious consideration. Having listened to everyone's complaints and suggestions, he reminded the people in the audience that while government could help in some areas, the city couldn't do everything. They would have to solve many of their own problems. He thanked them all for coming and asked them to vote for him on election day.

1. Why has Otis been holding public meetings instead of going on television, like Mr. Bascomb?
2. Why do you think so many people came to the meeting this afternoon?
3. Who is Bart Johnson? What did he say?
4. What's wrong with the Wickam Hotel?
5. What did Mr. Johnson want the city to do?
6. What was Mabel Brown concerned about? What did she say?
7. Who is Dr. Watkins? What did he say?
8. What was Gloria Cole concerned about? What did she say?
9. What was Olive Grove concerned about? What did she say?
10. What did the other members of the audience talk about?
11. What did Otis say about solving Wickam City's problems?

🔊 *Listen and practice.*

FRED: I enjoyed the meeting, Otis. It's good when people have a chance to speak their minds.

OTIS: What's on your mind, Fred?

FRED: Well, I'm mainly concerned about the young people of our town. There's too much juvenile delinquency. What happened to Olive Grove the other day is a typical example.

OTIS: The boys in that gang should be ashamed of themselves, robbing an old lady. I wonder what's wrong with them?

FRED: My guess is they're a bunch of bored kids. They probably have a lot of time on their hands and nothing to do, so they end up getting in trouble.

OTIS: It's a sad situation. What do you think can be done about it?

FRED: Well, first of all, we've got to take an interest in these boys. They can be helped, you know. Take Marty, for instance. When I first met him he was always getting into trouble, a real juvenile delinquent.

OTIS: What happened?

FRED: I started spending time with him, trying to help him with his problems, and teaching him things, like how to play sports. You should see Marty now; he's really changed. He's much better than before.

OTIS: That's wonderful, Fred. It seems like you're getting good results with the neighborhood boys.

FRED: Well, having been a juvenile delinquent myself, I understand their problems. Many of these kids come from broken homes, and they feel no one cares about them. All they really need is a little attention. That's why I spend time with them playing ball in the park.

OTIS: That's one of the reasons I've been fighting to save the park, so the kids of Wickam City will have a place to play.

FRED: I really appreciate what you're doing, Otis. But the boys need more than a park. They need a place of their own, where they can feel at home, a place where they can get help if they need it. What they really need is a boys' club.

OTIS: And you'd like to be in charge of starting it, right?

FRED: Yes, I would.

OTIS: Well, it's a big job, Fred, and they say you don't like to work.

FRED: I guess I got that reputation because most jobs seem boring to me, especially office jobs. But this is something different. I'll be working with kids, and I'll be outdoors most of the time.

OTIS: I believe you can do it, Fred. You seem to have plenty of confidence.

FRED: Sure, but it's not going to be easy. It takes a lot of money to start a boys' club. I tried to get help from Mr. Bascomb, but he wasn't interested. He said a boys' club wouldn't be good for the economy.

OTIS: I guess he doesn't like nonprofit organizations. They don't produce any tax money for the city.

FRED: It's really discouraging, Otis. There are times when I feel the boys' club is a lost cause.

OTIS: Don't worry, Fred. Your efforts haven't been wasted. You've got me on your side. If I become mayor, I'll do everything I can to help you start a boys' club.

FRED: That's great, Otis. I knew I could count on you. Now all you have to do is get elected.

PRACTICE • *Change the sentences using **having**.*

> He had spent a lot of time with them and understood their problems.
> **Having spent a lot of time with them, he understood their problems.**
>
> He had lived in the same neighborhood and knew what it was like.
> **Having lived in the same neighborhood, he knew what it was like.**

1. She had saved her money and was able to buy some new furniture.
2. He had lost his keys and couldn't get in the house.
3. We had talked over the situation and knew what to do.
4. I had spent all my money and had to stay home last weekend.
5. She had seen the movie three times and could describe it very well.
6. He had lost the tennis game and was very angry with himself.
7. He had done his best and had nothing to be ashamed of.
8. They had missed breakfast and were very hungry.
9. She had worked hard all day and needed a rest.
10. He had passed the test and felt like celebrating.
11. We had heard the good news and were very happy for him.
12. She had lived in Paris for several years and could speak French very well.

WRITTEN EXERCISE 1 • *Complete the sentences using past participles as adjectives.*

> Many candidates break their promises. We're tired of _broken_ promises.
>
> Mr. Bascomb has proven his ability many times. He's a man of _proven_ ability.

1. They scheduled the meeting for 5:00 P.M. It was the last _____ meeting of the day.

2. He got the results he had expected. He got the _____ results.

3. The newspapers favor him to win the election. He's the _____ candidate.

4. You should type that report before you send it in. They expect a _____ report.

5. You wasted your time on that last effort. It was a _____ effort.

6. Show me the report when you've finished it. I want to see the _____ report.

7. The girl next door doesn't like to fry fish. She hates the smell of _____ fish.

8. Her expression shows that she worries a lot. She has a _____ expression.

9. She admits that she's a failure. She's an _____ failure.

10. Her parents didn't give her the name Olive Oil. It isn't her _____ name.

11. They bought a car that someone else had used. It was a _____ car.

12. They didn't want to rent a car. It's too expensive driving a _____ car.

WRITTEN EXERCISE 2 • *Practice making sentences with participial adjectives using the words below.*

> trusted friend _Mr. Grubb is a trusted friend._
>
> crowded bus _Have you ever been on a crowded bus?_
>
> frightened woman _The frightened woman ran out of the theater._

1. qualified person _____

2. bored housewife _____

3. broken heart _____

4. drunk driver(s) _____

5. fried potatoes _____

6. stolen property _____

7. used car _____

8. worried look _____

9. written examination _____

This year's mayoral contest between Otis and Mr. Bascomb is turning out to be one of the most exciting campaigns in the history of Wickam City. In the beginning, Mr. Bascomb was favored to win by a wide margin. He had the full support of the business community and was easily the better known candidate. Recently, however, Otis has been catching up with Mr. Bascomb and now stands an even chance of winning the election.

In spite of all the campaign activity, including hundreds of speeches and public appearances by both candidates, almost 30 percent of the electorate is still undecided about who to vote for. To help the voters make up their minds, the City Council last Friday asked Otis and Mr. Bascomb to hold a second debate. Both candidates agreed that a second debate was necessary, but they disagreed about where it should be held. Mr. Bascomb favored the Chamber of Commerce because of its calm, businesslike atmosphere. Otis complained that the Chamber of Commerce, with a capacity of only two hundred, was much too small for the most important event of the campaign. He wanted the debate to be held at City Park, so everyone could attend. Of course, Mr. Bascomb opposed the idea. He said it would give Otis an unfair advantage since his whole campaign was based on saving the park. Finally, the two men agreed to debate each other on the steps of City Hall. They would meet at 2:00 P.M. on Monday, November 5, the day before the election.

As the time for the second debate drew near, Mr. Bascomb started feeling nervous. He knew that Otis was better at speaking in front of large audiences and would have the advantage of being younger and better looking. He was also aware that the winner of the second debate would probably win the election. On Sunday night, Mr. Bascomb was so nervous he couldn't sleep. He lay awake for hours worrying about the debate. When he finally did fall asleep, he had a nightmare. He dreamed that he made a fool of himself in his debate with Otis and everyone was laughing at him. He woke up in such a fearful state that he couldn't get back to sleep again.

All too soon it was Monday afternoon, just a few minutes before the start of the debate, and Mr. Bascomb was looking at himself in Barbara's hand mirror.

"Do you think I look OK, Barbara?" asked Mr. Bascomb anxiously. "Or do you think I would photograph better if I cut off the mustache?"

Barbara was busy sorting the pages of Mr. Bascomb's speech, which he had been working on right up to the last minute.

"In your case, Mr. Bascomb," she said, "I don't think it really makes any difference."

"Thanks a lot, Barbara," he growled. "You're beginning to sound just like Anne used to. But seriously, do you think I'm too formally dressed? Maybe I should wear leather and earrings to appeal to the younger voters. I don't want them to think that I haven't kept up with the times."

Barbara looked surprised. "Mr. Bascomb, I thought as a candidate you stressed the issues and not appearances. Besides, I just saw Otis and he's very well dressed in a conservative gray suit."

"You just saw Otis!" said Mr. Bascomb, more worried than ever. "How does he look? Is he nervous? Is he sweating?"

"No, Mr. Bascomb, he looks relaxed and natural, and he wishes you good luck in the debate," Barbara answered. "And now let's go, Mr. Bascomb, or you're going to be late, and that wouldn't look good for the candidate who stands for responsible city government."

Mr. Bascomb had butterflies in his stomach, but he knew it was too late for second thoughts. Not wanting to back out at the last minute, he picked up his speech, straightened his tie, and started out for City Hall.

Arriving at City Hall, Mr. Bascomb and Barbara found a large crowd already gathered. There was no time for Mr. Bascomb to answer any questions from the press as it was already two o'clock and the debate was about to begin. Mr. Bascomb climbed up the steps. The TV lights were very hot. He could hardly hear anything as he and Otis were being introduced. The moderator, Dr. Pasto, explained that each candidate would have fifteen minutes to state his position on the issues. This introductory period was to be followed by a question-and-answer session with members of the local press, after which each candidate would have five minutes to sum up.

Otis was the first to speak. He looked calm and relaxed as he stood up to address the audience. Mr. Bascomb, sitting a few feet away, looked very nervous and uncomfortable.

"My fellow citizens," said Otis, "this election is your opportunity to choose the kind of city you would like to live in. Our main concern should be the quality of life in Wickam City, and our first priority should be to protect the environment. I feel it would be a grave mistake for us to build a toy factory in City Park, as Mr. Bascomb suggests. The park should be kept for everyone to enjoy."

Suddenly a large number of people started clapping and cheering. Otis really knew how to stir up a crowd, thought Mr. Bascomb, green with envy. What little confidence he had was disappearing rapidly.

"Wickam City has greater potential for tourism than for industry," Otis went on. "We have some of the most beautiful scenery in the state, but we're losing the tourist trade because we don't have a single first-class hotel in good condition."

Many people in the audience nodded their heads in agreement. "I suggest we rebuild the Wickam Hotel," said Otis, "and make it an attractive place for tourists to stay. Increased tourism will provide more jobs and tax money for the city. We can use the money to finance badly needed social programs, such as a day care center and a boys' club." Otis made a few more remarks about his plans for improving education, transportation, and medical care in Wickam City. He sat down to the sound of clapping hands and cheering voices. Mr. Bascomb felt sick.

Now it was Mr. Bascomb's turn. His knees were shaking as he stood up. His throat felt dry. He was so nervous that he couldn't hold on to his speech. "Ladies and gentlemen," he said, "I realize that building a toy factory in City Park is a controversial issue. But let me explain why I'm in favor of it. The two main problems facing Wickam City today are high taxes and unemployment. The toy factory will provide hundreds of jobs while making it possible to lower your taxes. It's unrealistic to think we could achieve these goals by encouraging tourism. There are other towns in this area that are better equipped to handle the tourist trade than Wickam City. Rebuilding the Wickam Hotel is an expensive proposition and a risk that we cannot afford to take. On the other hand, the toy factory would be financed entirely by a company in Chicago. We wouldn't have to spend a dime, and we could be sure of the results."

A few people in the audience started clapping, but Mr. Bascomb couldn't hear them. "I have nothing against social programs," he went on. "But they cost a lot of money, and where is the money going to come from? Do you really want to pay higher taxes in order to have a boys' club and a day care center? Are you willing to have the government spend even more of your hard-earned money? I don't think social programs are something the government should do for the people, but something the people should do for themselves."

Mr. Bascomb looked out at the audience. There was total silence. It seemed as if no one there was on his side. He even thought he heard people laughing at him, just like in his nightmare. Fortunately, he was near the end of his speech. He finished by telling the audience about his plans for improving the economy. He reminded them that the only way to win the battle against rising taxes and inflation was to reduce government spending, and this could only be done with the help of the people. Finally, his time finished, he slumped down in his chair. He was certain that he had made a mess of his speech and was surprised to hear many people cheering.

Later, after the question-and-answer period and the summing up, Mr. Bascomb found himself face-to-face with Otis. He shook his hand and said, "Congratulations, Otis! I really admire the way you handle yourself in front of a crowd. I wish I had half your self-confidence and poise."

Otis grinned and shook his head in astonishment. "But Mr. Bascomb, I was going to say the same thing to you. As for me, I was so scared I could hardly stand up. I couldn't remember a thing I wanted to say, and you sounded so convincing, *I* almost decided to vote for *you*!"

STORY QUESTIONS

1. Why is it impossible to predict who will win the race for mayor of Wickam City?
2. Why did the City Council ask Otis and Mr. Bascomb to hold a second debate?
3. What advantages did Otis have in debating Mr. Bascomb?
4. Why did Mr. Bascomb have trouble sleeping Sunday night?
5. What happened when he finally fell asleep? What did he dream?
6. Why was Mr. Bascomb worried about his appearance on the day of the debate?
7. Who was the first man to speak in the debate?
8. Why is Otis opposed to building a toy factory in City Park?
9. What would Otis do to make life better for the people of Wickam City?
10. Where would he get the money to pay for his social programs?
11. Why is Mr. Bascomb in favor of building a toy factory in City Park?
12. What did Mr. Bascomb say about social programs and the role of the government?
13. Do you agree with Mr. Bascomb? Why or why not?
14. Which candidate do you think is better, Otis or Mr. Bascomb? Why?

READING

LETTERS TO THE DAILY NEWS

Juvenile Crime

Last week I was robbed by a gang a block from my house. They grabbed my handbag and ran off with my money. The boys who robbed me couldn't have been more than fourteen years old. It's just incredible what's happened to our community. This used to be such a quiet, peaceful place. I never thought I'd live to see the day when I'd be afraid to walk to the market.

Olive Grove

Increase in Bus Fare

I'm outraged by the recent increase in the bus fare from .90¢ to $1.25. People living on modest incomes can't afford to pay $55 a month just to go to work. How can the politicians justify a 40 percent increase in the bus fare when so many people are struggling to make ends meet? Instead of giving themselves raises, the politicians should use our tax money to make public transportation affordable for everyone.

Sebastian Humperdink

FREE RESPONSE

1. Do the complaints in these letters sound familiar to you?
2. What do people worry about where you live?
3. Is crime a serious problem in your city? What about gangs?
4. Have you ever been robbed? If so, how did it happen?
5. Do you think the police are doing a good job of fighting crime in your city?
6. How good is public transportation where you live? How could it be improved?
7. What are some of the needs of your city? How would you deal with these problems?
8. If you were the mayor of your city, what would you do to make it a better place to live?

COMPOSITION • *Working with a partner, write a letter to your local newspaper about a problem in your city. Try to suggest a possible solution.*

WRITTEN EXERCISE 1 • *Complete the sentences using the correct participle of the verb in parentheses.*

> He had a *worried* expression on his face. (worry)
> Nobody likes to be on the *losing* side of an argument. (lose)

1. The _____ man couldn't find a good lawyer to defend him. (accuse)

2. He had very few _____ arguments. (convince)

3. He was an _____ liar. (admit)

4. I'm sorry to give you such _____ news. (disappoint)

5. There are a lot of _____ mothers in our neighborhood. (work)

6. They're tired of empty speeches and _____ promises. (break)

7. No one seems to have any _____ ideas for improving the city. (excite)

8. We need a man of _____ ability. (prove)

9. He should be intelligent and have a good _____ voice. (speak)

10. He shouldn't be afraid of a long and _____ campaign. (tire)

11. If he loses the election, he can take an _____ vacation. (extend)

12. We'll even provide him with a good _____ car for his trip. (use)

WRITTEN EXERCISE 2 • *Fill in the blanks with the most appropriate participial phrases from the list below. Each participial phrase may be used only once.*

looking up at the sky	pouring himself another cup	pointing to his watch
taking off her shoes	running after her friends	pushing away her plate
reaching for an aspirin	turning on the radio	opening the window

> "This coffee is delicious," said Tino, *pouring himself another cup.*

1. "I can't eat any more food," said Barbara, _____.

2. "Let's listen to some music," said Peter, _____.

3. "I'm going to lie down," said Maria, _____.

4. "There's too much cigarette smoke in here," said Anne, _____.

5. "I've got a terrible headache," said Johnnie, _____.

6. "It's getting late," said Albert, _____.

7. "It's going to rain," said Jimmy, _____.

8. "Wait for me," said Linda, _____.

PAIR WORK • *Listen to the telephone conversations below. Write down the key words you hear in each conversation. Then write a summary of that conversation with your partner.*

Key words for conversation 1:

car for sale	four thousand
good condition	see car

Gloria called Nick's Garage about the **car** they had **for sale.** The man told her the car was in **good condition.** They were asking **four thousand** for it. Gloria decided to go and **see** the **car.**

1. Gloria

2. Mr. Farley

3. Gladys

4. Mr. Ripken

5. Carlos

6. Mrs. Golo

ROLE PLAY • *With your partner, choose one of the situations above and have a conversation similar to the conversation you heard on tape. Feel free to improvise and use your own information. Role play your conversation before the class.*

Was it only a coincidence that Anne appeared at the wishing well just after Johnnie had made his wish, or was there something more that caused her to appear? Some people feel that when things like this happen, it is not just a coincidence, but a manifestation of some higher power or order where all things, including our thoughts, come together. "Ridiculous!" say others. "That's all superstition." Perhaps—but let's take a further look before we jump to conclusions.

We all know that some things exist even though we cannot see them with our own eyes: electricity, love, pain, the sun on a cloudy day. And many of us have had the experience of *déjà vu*—the feeling of having been in a specific place and situation before. And most of us have performed various superstitious rites, such as blowing out the candles on a birthday cake or crossing our fingers for luck. Many of us have had a dream about a friend or relative who we haven't seen in a long time, and then the person just happens to appear the next day.

Throughout history people have observed strange, unexplainable events and have wanted to know their cause and their meaning. Scientists have studied nature and have found perfect order in it, down to the smallest levels of existence. Psychologists are studying the human mind and making important discoveries. And yet, as deep as we go into things, there are always mysteries that lie just beyond our understanding. Within nature we have discovered a particle smaller than the electron, and through an abstract formula ($E = mc^2$) we have found the link between matter and energy. But in spite of all the scientific progress we have made, there are still happenings that we call "supernatural" because we do not understand them.

Do miracles as in biblical times still happen today? Some insist that they do. There are many people in the world today who, at one time in their lives, were declared terminally ill, but through prayer and faith have completely recovered without the help of medicine. There are recorded cases of people doing things that, under normal circumstances, would be absolutely impossible for them, such as the frail old woman who lifted a car off the ground when her grandchild was trapped under it. And of course there are cases of people who claim to have seen "visions" of other times and other worlds.

Sometimes we hear about coincidences that are so extraordinary we have to stop and ask ourselves, "What made such a strange thing happen?" For example, a friend says, "I haven't seen Mary in ten years. I dreamed about her last night, and she called me today." Is it just coincidence? Or is it something more? Of course, there are many mysteries in life that we may never understand. And many people are troubled because they don't have answers to these mysteries. But there is no need for despair, for as long as there is that force that brought Anne and Johnnie back together, there is hope for the world. That force is love.

1. When was the last time you had a coincidence in your life? What happened?
2. Have you ever experienced *déjà vu*?
3. What are some things that we know exist without our ability to see them?
4. Do you believe in miracles?
5. Can you give any examples of miracles?

When most of us get sick we go to a doctor, get a prescription, and take a drug. With certain types of health problems, drugs can achieve beneficial results. However, there are many chronic illnesses that don't respond well to pills. Common ailments such as insomnia, backaches, and depression are stress-related, and they are directly affected by the patient's state of mind. To provide the most effective therapy for these conditions, it is necessary to address the psychological needs of the patient as part of the treatment. For this reason, a growing number of doctors are examining the connection between healing and spirituality. They are discovering that love, laughter, positive thoughts, and faith are good for one's health.

Love is the most powerful stimulant to the immune system. Love boosts our spirits and motivates us to get well. The truth is, love can heal.

Laughter relieves pain and helps us relax. A well-developed sense of humor counteracts the negative emotions that can cause and aggravate illness.

When we picture ourselves getting well, we help our body to heal itself because the body responds to the mind's messages. **Positive thoughts** activate beneficial hormones that promote healing.

Studies show that people who have **faith** in a benevolent higher power have lower blood pressure, less heart disease, lower rates of depression, and generally better health than those who don't believe.

This evidence supports the view that we can have greater success in overcoming illness and staying healthy if we combine the best of modern medicine with a positive lifestyle.

1. What does it mean to have a positive lifestyle?
2. What are some of the ways that a positive lifestyle can contribute to good health?
3. Are you doing the things you should to stay healthy? Give some examples.

VOCABULARY

achieve
agreement
appeal (v.)
atmosphere

balance (n.)
battle (n.)
beneficial
bore (v.)

cause (n.)
citizen
claim (v.)
conservative
consideration
contribute
courteous

day care
delirious
dime
dining hall
disease
dive (v.)

effective
efficient
effort
entirely
examine

faith
fever
finance (v.)
fool (n.)

goal

head
hormone
horrible

immune system
inflation

justify

laughter
lifestyle

mainly
meaning
member

miracle
motivate
mustache

nasty
nightmare

obligation

penny
percentage
please (v.)
potential (n.)
prescription
press (n.)
priority

rapidly
reduce

reputation
respond
result (n.)

self-confidence
solve
struggle (v.)
suggest
sweat (v.)

thankful
therapy
treatment
TV commercial
typical

unfair
unrealistic

wish (n.)

EXPRESSIONS

to be aware of something
to be in charge of something
to make a fool of oneself

to be damaged
to be based on
to be outraged

to speak out
to go all out
to back out

to be out of work
to make ends meet
to feel at home

to end up
to put up with
to catch up with

in your case
face-to-face
standing room only

He was green with envy.
He hasn't been himself lately.
He has nothing against social programs.

I admire the way you handle yourself.
They have a lot of time on their hands.
It doesn't make any difference.

He had butterflies in his stomach.
It was too late for second thoughts.

He's out of his mind.
What's on your mind?
It's good to speak your mind.

Shut up!
I can't help it!
I guess so.

THE PRESENT PARTICIPLE
Present Participles Used as Adjectives

His announcement surprised everyone.	He made a surprising announcement.
Your sister bores me.	You have a boring sister.

Participial Phrases Used as Sentence Modifiers

She waved good-bye and got on the bus.	Waving good-bye, she got on the bus.
I looked up and saw a black cat.	Looking up, I saw a black cat.

He sat on the bench	feeding the pigeons. talking to some children. reading a magazine. eating a sandwich. listening to the radio.

THE PAST PARTICIPLE
Past Participles Used as Adjectives

The man has changed a lot in the last year.	He is a changed man now.
We got the results that we had expected.	We got the expected results.

Participial Phrases Used as Sentence Modifiers

She had gotten the job and was very happy.	Having gotten the job, she was very happy.
He had failed twice and felt like giving up.	Having failed twice, he felt like giving up.

Chapter

TOPICS
American holidays
Proverbs
Television
Lying

GRAMMAR
Review

FUNCTIONS
Expressing possibility and probability
Saying good-bye
Making recommendations
Agreeing and disagreeing

It is election day in Wickam City. The polls opened at eight o'clock in the morning and will remain open until eight at night. Everyone is interested in the outcome of the election and a heavy turnout is expected. So far the public opinion surveys have been unable to pick a clear winner. Opinion is evenly divided, feelings are strong, and sometimes even old friends disagree sharply over who should be Wickam City's next mayor.

At Nick's Garage, out on the edge of town, Sam and Mabel have stopped to put some gas in their old truck. "Hurry up, Nick," says Sam, "we haven't got all day!"

"What's your rush, Sam?" asks Nick. "Did Mabel leave a cake in the oven?"

"No," answers Mabel, "but we've got to get over to the schoolhouse and vote before the polls close. We promised that nice young Otis fellow our vote."

"I voted early this morning to avoid the crowds," says Nick. "But I used my head and voted for Bascomb. I figure that as a businessman I had no other choice. Besides, I'm too old to use the park, and so are the two of you."

"Voting for Bascomb is more a case of *losing* your head than of *using* it," says Sam, "and, as for being too old to use the park, speak for yourself, Nick. Mabel and I still enjoy a little stroll on moonlit nights."

Mabel blushes. "And think of your children, Nick. With the park gone, where will they play?"

"I *am* thinking of my children, Mabel," sighs Nick. "I need to do more business so I can pay for their education. That's why I voted for Bascomb."

Sam says, "If you want to do more business, Nick, why don't you start now by putting some gas in our tank? Or do you plan to keep us here all day so we can't vote for Otis?"

Quite a few people have gathered at Martinoli's. They are discussing the election and the events of the day. Barbara is taking Tino's place waiting on tables while he runs across the street to vote.

"Well, Barbara," Nancy Paine is saying, "I guess there's no doubt about how you voted, is there?"

"What do you mean, Nancy?" asks Barbara.

"I mean, since you work for Bascomb, you must have felt obliged to give him your vote."

"Why, Nancy Paine, I'm surprised at you! How could you even imagine such a thing? The fact that I work for Mr. Bascomb has nothing to do with my private life."

"Do you mean to say that you voted for Otis?" asks Nancy. "I find that hard to believe."

"It's really none of your business who I voted for, Nancy Paine," replied Barbara angrily, "but yes, as a matter of fact, I voted for Otis because I think he's the best man for the job."

Just then Peter sees Dr. Pasto walking by. "Dr. Pasto," he calls out, "come and have an iced tea with us and tell us who you voted for."

Dr. Pasto smiles and replies, "I'll happily accept your kind invitation to drink an iced tea, but as for telling you who I voted for, that, my friend, is a secret I shall carry to the grave."

"But Dr. Pasto," says Maria, "do you mean to say that you're afraid to tell us who you voted for?"

"My dear young lady," says Dr. Pasto, "it's not cowardice, but common sense. First, my firm conviction is that the secret ballot is the keystone of the democratic process. Second, experience has shown me that he who remains in silence gives neither displeasure to his friends nor comfort to his enemies."

"Oh, Dr. Pasto, that's silly," says Gloria. "We're all mature adults. We aren't going to let a little thing like a political disagreement come between friends."

Dr. Pasto merely smiles and gestures toward the sidewalk where Anne and Johnnie are passing by. They are having a heated argument and don't notice anyone around them. Anne is speaking.

"Oh Johnnie, how could you be so silly? You knew Otis was my candidate."

"That's right, Anne, he was *your* candidate, but I felt that Mr. Bascomb was better qualified to run the city." Johnnie was gesticulating wildly. "And who are you calling silly? The trouble with you is you never use your head."

"Don't shout at me."

"I'M NOT SHOUTING AT YOU!"

"Leave me alone. I never want to see you again."

"Likewise."

Dr. Pasto sips his iced tea. "That's politics," he says. "Have I made my point?"

Mr. Bascomb has been working hard at the bank all day, trying to catch up on all the work he didn't do during the campaign. Suddenly he realizes that it is very late. If he doesn't hurry, he won't arrive at the polls in time to vote. He rushes out of the bank just in time to see Barney pulling up to the curb in his taxi. He runs over and is about to open the door when a voice stops him.

"I'm sorry, Mr. Bascomb, but I believe this is my taxi." It's Otis!

"No, I'm sorry, Otis, but I saw Barney first. Besides, this is an emergency. I have only ten minutes to get over to the firehouse and vote."

"What a coincidence, Mr. Bascomb. I have just ten minutes to get over to the public school and vote. I've been so busy all day that I forgot to vote myself."

"Well," says Mr. Bascomb, "I guess we're both in the same boat. But what are we going to do? There isn't enough time for both of us to go to the polls."

"Look, Mr. Bascomb," says Otis. "I have an idea. Since there isn't enough time for both of us to vote and we can't decide who saw the taxi first, let's compromise by not voting."

"Why, of course," says Mr. Bascomb. "I was going to vote for myself, and you naturally were going to vote for yourself. If neither of us votes, it'll come out the same. This way no one will get hurt. Come on, Otis, let me treat you to a cup of coffee. So long, Barney."

"Politicians," mutters Barney under his breath as Otis and Mr. Bascomb walk off. "'This way no one gets hurt.' Humph! No one but me, that is. What about my fare?"

Outside the public school, Marty and Jenny watch the long line of people waiting to vote. "Gee," exclaims Jenny, "voting looks like fun! When I grow up I'm going to vote, too. I wish I were grown up now."

"Me too," says Marty. "Why don't they let kids vote? If you could vote, who would you vote for?"

STORY QUESTIONS

1. What are the people at Martinoli's talking about?
2. Why was Nancy surprised to hear that Barbara voted for Otis?
3. Why won't Dr. Pasto tell anyone who he voted for?
4. How do Anne and Johnnie prove Dr. Pasto's point about politics?
5. What is the coincidence involving Otis and Mr. Bascomb?
6. How do they resolve their problem?
7. Why doesn't it make any difference if they vote or not?
8. Why is Barney upset when Otis and Mr. Bascomb go off for a cup of coffee?
9. What does Jenny think about voting?
10. Who would you vote for, Otis or Mr. Bascomb? Why?

FREE RESPONSE 1 • *What do you think will happen if . . .*

1. Mr. Bascomb wins the election?
2. Otis wins the election?
3. They build a toy factory in City Park?
4. Mr. Bascomb finds out that Barbara voted for Otis?
5. Dr. Pasto runs for mayor four years from now?
6. Anne and Johnnie get married?

FREE RESPONSE 2 • *Suppose you were the mayor of the city where you are living now.*

1. What would you do to improve public transportation?
2. What would you do about pollution?
3. How would you provide more jobs?
4. What would you do about taxes?
5. What would you do about crime?
6. What would you do to help homeless people?
7. How would you improve education?
8. What else would you do and why?

PRACTICE • *Make sentences using the third conditional.*

He lost the debate.
He wouldn't have lost the debate if he had been more relaxed.

He didn't get elected.
He would have gotten elected if he hadn't lost the debate.

1. He didn't get the job.
2. She didn't marry him.
3. They lost their money.
4. We didn't help them.
5. I didn't go to the party.
6. He didn't pass the exam.
7. They missed the bus.
8. We got in trouble.

WRITTEN EXERCISE • *Complete the sentences using **must have been, might have been, should have been,** or **would have been,** whichever is the most appropriate.*

It was a very old house. It *must have been built* over ninety years ago.
(build)

We don't know why she left the party early. She *might have been tired*.
(tire)

1. I don't think she _____ if she had been more careful.
   (rob)

2. Who knows? She _____ just because she is a woman.
   (hold up)

3. She _____ because she didn't try to call for help.
   (frighten)

4. If you had been stopped by a man with a gun, you _____ too.
   (scare)

5. It's a good thing she didn't get into a fight. She _____.
   (hurt)

6. We're upset. We think she _____ a ride home from the party.
   (give)

7. If they had gone straight to the police, there's a chance she

   _____ by now.
   (rescue)

8. That letter wasn't written by her. It _____ by someone else.
   (write)

9. No one wanted to worry her family, but I think they _____
   the truth.
   (tell)

New Year's is one of the oldest and most universally observed holidays. In the United States, New Year's Eve is often the occasion for parties in people's homes, hotels, and restaurants. At midnight the New Year is welcomed with a lot of noise and merrymaking. For some people, New Year's is also a time to reflect and make resolutions for the coming year.

Independence Day, or the Fourth of July, is the greatest patriotic holiday in the United States. On July 4, 1776, America declared its independence from Great Britain. Americans celebrate the anniversary of this event with fireworks, parades, and patriotic speeches.

Thanksgiving Day is a national holiday celebrating the harvest and other blessings of the past year. It originated in the autumn of 1621, when the Indians joined the Pilgrims for a three-day festival of recreation and feasting. Americans celebrate Thanksgiving on the fourth Thursday of November by having a traditional dinner of turkey and pumpkin pie.

Christmas is a very important holiday in the United States. It celebrates the birth of Jesus Christ on December 25th. On this day, most families get together for a big dinner. They exchange presents and visit friends. On Christmas Eve, many Americans attend church services and sing Christmas carols.

DISCUSSION • *Do you celebrate any of these holidays in your country? Talk about some of your favorite holidays. Are there any special customs?*

 *Listen and practice.*

Joe is going to Florida to try out for a professional baseball team. He will be away for several weeks. Linda is seeing him off at the airport.

LINDA: Good luck, Joe. I hope you make the team.

JOE: Thanks, Linda.

LINDA: Joe . . .

JOE: Yes?

LINDA: Don't be too friendly with the girls in Florida.

JOE: Don't worry. I'm only going there to play baseball.

LINDA: I wish I could go with you.

JOE: So do I. I'll miss you, Linda.

LINDA: I'll miss you, too. Keep in touch.

JOE: Okay, I'll write soon. Take care of yourself.

LINDA: Bye-bye, Joe. Have a good trip.

JOE: Bye, Linda.

DIALOGUE QUESTIONS

1. Why is Joe going to Florida?
2. What does Linda wish she could do?
3. How often do you think Joe and Linda will call or write to each other?
4. Do you think Joe is lucky to have a girlfriend like Linda?
5. What do you think will happen when Joe gets back from Florida?

FREE RESPONSE

1. When was the last time you saw someone off?
2. Who was the person and where did you say good-bye?
3. Do you remember what you said to each other?
4. How did you feel?

ROLE PLAY • *Imagine you are at the airport. You are saying good-bye to a friend. Act out a conversation similar to the one between Joe and Linda.*

1. Birds of a feather flock together.

2. Don't cry over spilled milk.

3. Don't count your chickens before they hatch.

4. You can lead a horse to water, but you can't make him drink.

5. All work and no play makes Jack a dull boy.

6. Seeing is believing.

DISCUSSION • *Do you agree with these proverbs? Do you have similar proverbs in your country?*

WRITTEN EXERCISE • *Complete the sentences using the infinitive or the gerund form of the verb in parentheses.*

She was accused of (take) ___*taking*___ apples from Dr. Pasto's tree even though she wasn't tall enough (reach) ___*to reach*___ them.

1. He wanted something cool (drink) _____ after (work)

   _____ all day in the hot sun.

2. My girlfriend arranged (meet) _____ Mr. Bascomb by (tell)

   _____ his secretary that she was a reporter for the *Daily News*.

3. I consider Mr. Bascomb (be) _____ the best candidate and have asked

   all my friends (vote) _____ for him.

4. The woman next door seems (know) _____ a lot about politics and is

   very good at (get) _____ others (accept) _____ her ideas.

5. It's hard (believe) _____ that she can hold two jobs while (go)

   _____ to college.

6. Now that she lives in an apartment, she misses (not have) _____ a garden

   or (be) _____ able (play) _____ the piano late at night.

7. We warned her (be) _____ careful about (talk) _____

   to strangers.

8. Old Farnsworth doesn't have the nerve (quit) _____ his job without

   (talk) _____ to his wife about it first.

9. His daughter Josie promised (clean up) _____ the kitchen before

   (go out) _____ with her friends this afternoon.

10. They don't mind (wait) _____ as long as they get (see)

    _____ the five o'clock show.

11. It's too hot (have) _____ a picnic at the park, and we don't feel like (go)

    _____ to the lake.

12. You may be upset about the boys (take) _____ your things without (ask)

    _____ permission, but it isn't worth (lose) _____ your temper.

Listen and practice.

Mr. and Mrs. Golo would like to take a tour in the fall. At the moment they are talking to their travel agent, Mr. Winkle.

(1) MR. WINKLE: You've picked a good time to travel, Mr. and Mrs. Golo. I have some very interesting tours this fall.

(2) MRS. GOLO: Do you have any tours that go to unusual places, Mr. Winkle?

(3) MR. WINKLE: I can send you anywhere in the world. Where would you like to go?

(4) MRS. GOLO: Well, we've already been to Europe. On our next trip we'd like to go somewhere more exotic.

(5) MR. GOLO: We want to get away from the crowds and see something different.

(6) MR. WINKLE: Hmm. I know just the place for you. It's called Bake Island.

(7) MR. GOLO: I've never heard of it.

(8) MRS. GOLO: Where is it, Mr. Winkle?

(9) MR. WINKLE: It's in the Indian Ocean. You can see it on the globe.

(10) MR. GOLO: What is Bake Island like?

(11) MR. WINKLE: It's a wonderful place. It has good food, beautiful beaches, and sunny weather.

(12) MR. GOLO: How much is the tour, Mr. Winkle?

(13) MR. WINKLE: It's only twelve hundred dollars, and that includes all your meals.

(14) MRS. GOLO: Will we have much free time to go sightseeing?

(15) MR. WINKLE: You'll have all the free time you want. And there'll be an experienced guide to make sure that all your needs are taken care of.

(16) MR. GOLO: Okay, Mr. Winkle, you don't have to say any more. We've decided to take the tour.

(17) MR. WINKLE: You've made a wise decision. Very few people get a chance to visit a place as beautiful as Bake Island.

(18) MRS. GOLO: You make it sound very exciting, Mr. Winkle, like a great adventure.

(19) MR. WINKLE: I'm sure you'll never forget Bake Island, Mrs. Golo. It's in a class by itself.

WRITTEN EXERCISE • *Rewrite the preceding dialogue using reported speech.*

1. Mr. Winkle told Mr. and Mrs. Golo that they had picked a good time to travel. He had some interesting tours that fall.
2. Mrs. Golo asked him if he had any tours that went to unusual places.
3. Mr. Winkle said that he could . . .

PRACTICE • *Combine the sentences using* **so . . . (that)** *and* **such . . . (that).**

The tour was very cheap. We couldn't refuse.
The tour was so cheap (that) we couldn't refuse.

Bake Island was a small island. No one knew about it.
Bake Island was such a small island (that) no one knew about it.

1. Our travel agent said it's a wonderful place. Everyone has a good time there.
2. He said the islanders are very friendly. They make you feel right at home.
3. His arguments were very convincing. We all believed him.
4. When we got to the island, we were disappointed. We didn't know what to say.
5. The water was very dirty. You couldn't swim in it.
6. They gave us horrible food. We had to throw it out.
7. The souvenirs were very expensive. We didn't buy anything.
8. Our guide had a very unpleasant voice. Nobody could listen to him.
9. He said that Bake Island was becoming famous. Everyone wanted to go there.
10. His comments were ridiculous. We all laughed.
11. He was an incredible fool. He actually believed what he was saying.
12. It was an awful, frightening place. We couldn't wait to leave.

ROLE PLAY

Student A plays a travel agent. Student B plays a customer.
Situation 1: The customer has a lot of money and wants to take a deluxe tour.
  The travel agent recommends a special tour for rich travelers.
Situation 2: The customer has very little money. The travel agent recommends
  an inexpensive tour.

Can you live without TV? Have you ever tried? Even for a week? An organization called TV-Free America is campaigning for people to do just that—spend seven days without watching any television. As part of its campaign, TV-Free America is disseminating information about the harmful effects of watching too much television. According to the studies, the "idiot box" encourages passivity, undermines family life, and imparts the wrong values.

People who spend a lot of time in front of the tube are spectators, not doers. Watching TV is easy; it requires no mental or physical effort. Just push a button and you can be entertained by a stream of dazzling images. It's the fast, modern way to relax and fight boredom at the same time. But watching TV is like taking a cheap drug with serious side effects. It's the substitution of second-hand experience for actual living. We are more comfortable talking about the escapades of characters in TV soap operas than we are in dealing with our problems in real life. The more we watch television, the less likely we are to do anything that will enrich our lives.

We hear a lot of reports about the negative influence of TV on families, especially children. If you think the reports are exaggerated, take a good look at children in our society. Do TV-loving kids have hobbies or passionate interests or dreams? Do they learn how to amuse themselves or how to get along with others? In the average American family, kids talk to their parents about the things that really matter to them less than six minutes a day. On that same day, they absorb television values for more than four hours. By the time the average child finishes elementary school in America, that child has probably seen 8,000 murders on television. Upon graduating from high school, the average child will have spent more time watching TV than in school. Most parents would like to limit their children's TV viewing, but they have come to rely on the TV set as a baby-sitter to keep the kids occupied while the parents relax or do other things. To complicate matters, most adults have the same addiction to television that kids have. We have become a nation of addicts.

Our addiction to television would be less serious if there were more quality programs on TV—more programs that are inspiring and uplifting. But what incentive is there to produce quality programs when it's so much easier and more profitable to turn out junk? TV producers know from experience that nothing sells like sex and violence: "So what if it's trash? We're only giving the public what it wants. Besides, it's only entertainment." That's how the producers respond to criticism from concerned citizens. But are the producers underestimating the influence of television in our lives? Many critics of television think so. They argue that television is a powerful force in our culture, and that out of culture comes behavior. Surely, the negative values we absorb from television can only have a negative effect on our thoughts and actions. Moreover, the American people seem to support this view. Seventy-two percent of Americans believe that TV violence helps precipitate real-life mayhem. And, 92 percent of Americans believe that TV commercials aimed at children make them too materialistic. TV commercials give children (and adults) the false impression that buying things is the way to be happy.

As bad as television is, the biggest problem may not be the quality of its programming, but the amount of time it takes away from crucial things in our lives: family, friends, study, reading, thought. The answer, ultimately, is to cut down on the amount of television we watch and fill our lives with other activities: talking to friends, listening to music, enjoying nature, playing sports, thinking, creating, doing! To get started, we have to take the long view and remind ourselves that no one ever lay on his deathbed wishing he'd watched more "Matlock."

1. What is TV-Free America trying to do?
2. What are the harmful effects of watching too much television?
3. Why do people spend so much time watching TV?
4. How is TV harmful to children?
5. How much time do American kids spend talking to their parents about important things?
6. Why don't parents make their children watch less TV?
7. Why don't producers give us more quality TV programs?
8. Why is there so much sex and violence on American TV?
9. What do you think is the worst thing about watching too much TV?
10. What are some other activities we can do in our leisure time?

FREE RESPONSE

1. How many hours of television do you watch every day?
2. How would you rate the quality of most TV programs in your country?
3. How does television in your country compare with television in the United States?
4. Do people in your country complain about too much sex and violence on TV?
5. Do you think there is a connection between TV violence and real-life violence?
6. Do you think the government should take some TV programs off the air?
7. Can producers broadcast anything they want in your country?
8. If you were a TV producer, what kind of programs would you produce?
9. How would your life be different if you didn't have a TV set?
10. Do you think this would be a better world if there were no television? Why?

GROUP WORK • *Talk about television. Do you agree or disagree with the opinions below? Explain why.*

- Watching TV is a waste of time.
- Watching TV is a good way to relax and have fun.
- There is too much sex and violence on television.
- Television shows life the way it really is.
- We can learn a lot from watching TV.

We all like to think of ourselves as honest people who try to tell the truth. But we have to admit that there are times when almost everyone lies. For example, we often tell "white lies" when it would be considered rude or offensive to "tell it like it is." Telling a lie may or may not be a terrible thing, depending on the situation. Here are four of the most common types of lies:

1. *Lying to protect someone's feelings.* You want to avoid saying what you really think because it might hurt another person's feelings, so you say something complimentary, a white lie that will make the person feel good.

2. *Lying to protect yourself.* You want to get out of an uncomfortable or "sticky" situation, so you say something to make people think you're innocent. Criminals always deny responsibility in order to get away with something.

3. *Lying to impress others.* You want to be popular, gain approval, or sound important, so you say something that will make people think well of you.

4. *Lying to make a polite excuse.* You want to avoid doing something that you find unpleasant, so you make up a polite excuse that will satisfy the other person.

When it comes to lying, the best advice for people with good intentions may be to follow the Golden Rule: "Do unto others as you would have them do unto you."

FREE RESPONSE

1. Do you think people should always tell the truth?
2. Have you ever told a white lie? If so, what was the reason?
3. Has anyone ever lied to you or about you? What did they say? How did you feel?
4. What do you think is the most common type of lie?

GROUP WORK • *Talk about each picture below. Use these questions and others of your own.*

- Why is the speaker lying?
- Do you think it's OK to lie in this situation?
- What would happen if the speaker told the truth?
- What would you say if you were the speaker?

 LISTENING • *Listen to the speakers. Then listen to the responses they get from the other people. Do you think the other people believe the speakers or not?*

ROLE PLAY • *Choose one of the situations above and make up a conversation. Role play the conversation before the class.*

FREE RESPONSE

1. When was the last time you ran into an old friend? Where and how did it happen? Did you make plans to meet again? What did you say to each other?
2. How do you greet your friends—with a handshake, a hug, or a kiss? Do you greet everyone the same way? Explain.
3. Have you met any new people recently? Where and how?
4. Do you think it's important to be on time? When was the last time you were late for something? Why were you late?
5. Have you ever been blamed for something you didn't do? What was it?
6. Have you ever missed a good opportunity? What was it?
7. Do you have any regrets? Can you think of anything you should or shouldn't have done?
8. Have you ever made a New Year's resolution? What was it?
9. What are your plans for the future?
10. What do you hope will happen this year or next year?

VOCABULARY

anniversary	festival	outcome
	firm (adj.)	
behavior		patriotic
blame (v.)	gesture (v.)	process (n.)
		protect
comfort (n.)	impress	
comment (n.)	independence	reflect
compromise (v.)	Indian Ocean	responsibility
culture		
	likewise	secret
democratic		spectator
disagreement	mature	survey (n.)
dull	murder (n.)	
		values
effect	need (n.)	
enemy	nor	wise
event		

EXPRESSIONS

What a coincidence!
We're in the same boat.
We haven't got all day.

It's common sense.
Have I made my point?
It's none of your business.

Speak for yourself!
Use your head!
I'm surprised at you.

What's your rush?
I'll miss you.
She's taking his place.

It's in a class by itself.
They make you feel right at home.

to keep in touch
to see someone off
to hurt someone's feelings

to feel obliged
as a matter of fact
depending on the situation

1. When she left the building, she had the feeling she _____.
   - A. was watched
   - B. has been watched
   - C. was being watched
   - D. had been watched

2. Two men _____ on the bridge were injured yesterday afternoon.
   - A. working
   - B. work
   - C. worked
   - D. were working

3. For three days we _____ the living room, and we still haven't finished.
   - A. paint
   - B. are painting
   - C. have to paint
   - D. have been painting

4. Has Barbara typed the letter yet?
   Yes, she _____ it a long time ago.
   - A. typed
   - B. has typed
   - C. was typing
   - D. has been typing

5. I prefer reading _____ television.
   - A. than watch
   - B. to watch
   - C. to watching
   - D. than watching

6. If Otis _____ mayor, he will save the park.
   - A. will become
   - B. becomes
   - C. is becoming
   - D. became

7. Please call Gloria when you _____ home.
   - A. get
   - B. will get
   - C. get to
   - D. are getting

8. We will have a picnic on Saturday _____ it rains.
   - A. if
   - B. even though
   - C. although
   - D. unless

9. I can't find my sister. Do you know _____?
   - A. where is she
   - B. somewhere she is
   - C. where she is
   - D. is she anywhere

10. She was in a hurry. That's _____ she forgot her keys.
    - A. why
    - B. when
    - C. where
    - D. because

11. Do you think our team will win the big game on Sunday?
    I don't know. They _____ win.
    - A. would
    - B. will
    - C. can
    - D. might

12. We love to play tennis, but if they close the park we _____ play tennis any more.
    - A. can't
    - B. couldn't
    - C. won't be able to
    - D. won't have to

13. Jenny's mother allowed her _____ to the party last night.
    - A. go
    - B. to go
    - C. going
    - D. went

14. Mr. Dole _____ buy a car, so he could drive to work.
    - A. has to
    - B. will have to
    - C. has had to
    - D. had to

15. This box is _____ heavy that I can't lift it.
    - A. very
    - B. too
    - C. so
    - D. enough

16. Judy isn't _____ to vote.
    - A. so old
    - B. very old
    - C. enough old
    - D. old enough

17. If I were you, I _____ more exercise.
    - A. would get
    - B. will get
    - C. can get
    - D. shall get

18. If they _____ harder, they would succeed.
    - A. could try
    - B. tried
    - C. try
    - D. had tried

19. Mabel was making dinner when Sam _____ home.
    - A. came
    - B. was coming
    - C. has come
    - D. comes

20. The telegram _____ at nine o'clock yesterday morning.
    - A. has arrived
    - B. was arriving
    - C. arrived
    - D. had arrived

21. I was doing the shopping while you
_____ tennis.

A. played   C. have played
B. were playing   D. have been playing

22. I wonder when _____ home.

A. is she coming   C. she is coming
B. will she come   D. can she come

23. They are giving away _____ of their old furniture.

A. any   C. few
B. many   D. some

24. Sandy didn't meet Otis, _____?

A. she did   C. didn't she
B. did she   D. she didn't

25. There is only one way to win the battle _____ inflation.

A. with   C. for
B. against   D. from

26. Some of the tenants are upset because the landlord won't _____ the building.

A. keep off   C. keep up
B. keep on   D. keep up with

27. They took a rest after they _____ the yard.

A. had cleaned up   C. would clean up
B. were cleaning up   D. have cleaned up

28. Ms. Blake _____ the bus before the accident took place.

A. had gotten off   C. has gotten off
B. was getting off   D. would get off

29. Fred _____ better as soon as he had eaten dinner.

A. would feel   C. felt
B. will feel   D. could feel

30. They had their car _____ at Nick's Garage.

A. repairing   C. repaired
B. to repair   D. repair

31. Barbara made Tino _____ the kitchen.

A. to paint   C. painted
B. painting   D. paint

32. Marty wishes he _____ the exam.

A. will pass   C. was passing
B. had passed   D. passed

33. Jenny said, "I'll wash the dishes."
What did she say?

She said she _____ the dishes.

A. would wash   C. shall wash
B. will wash   D. could wash

34. "Are you leaving, Sam?" asked Mabel.
What did she ask him?

She asked him if he _____.

A. is leaving   C. leaves
B. was leaving   D. would leave

35. "How have you been, Mona?" asked Fred.
What did he ask her?

He asked her how _____.

A. she is   C. she had been
B. was she   D. had she been

36. If it keeps on raining, the game may _____.

A. delay   C. have delayed
B. be delayed   D. have to delay

37. Linda is doing her homework now. She _____ TV an hour from now.

A. watches   C. would watch
B. shall watch   D. will be watching

38. The library _____ since last Wednesday.

A. has been closed   C. closed
B. was closed   D. is closed

39. John's wife _____ dinner by the time he gets home.

A. is going to eat   C. will eat
B. will have eaten   D. would eat

40. We don't have a car, _____ we take the bus to work.

  A. since
  B. in order to
  C. although
  D. so

41. Maria took time to help me _____ she was very busy.

  A. since
  B. because
  C. although
  D. so

42 They were looking for a good _____ car.

  A. use
  B. used
  C. to use
  D. using

43. They will work overtime if they _____ for it.

  A. get paid
  B. will get paid
  C. would get paid
  D. have gotten paid

44. Sam would have met Otis if he _____ to the meeting.

  A. goes
  B. went
  C. had gone
  D. would go

45. He is very tired. He _____ hard today.

  A. might have worked
  B. must have worked
  C. should have worked
  D. would have worked

46. Gloria was late to work. She _____ a taxi instead of waiting for the bus.

  A. would have taken
  B. might have taken
  C. must have taken
  D. should have taken

47. No one realized the letter was important, or it _____ thrown out.

  A. would have been
  B. wouldn't have been
  C. should have been
  D. might have been

48. I don't care if we go to the beach or not.

  _____.

  A. It's up to you
  B. Mind your own business
  C. We haven't got all day
  D. It isn't worth it

49. He is a good employee because

  _____.

  A. he doesn't know his place
  B. you can put yourself in his shoes
  C. you can always count on him
  D. it's the least he can do

50. She lost her job yesterday.

  _____.

  A. We are proud of her
  B. I can't stand her
  C. I believe in her
  D. I feel sorry for her

Appendix

INFINITIVE	PAST TENSE	PAST PARTICIPLE	INFINITIVE	PAST TENSE	PAST PARTICIPLE
be	was/were	been	let	let	let
beat	beat	beaten	lie	lay	lain
become	became	become	light	lit	lit
bet	bet	bet	lose	lost	lost
bite	bit	bitten	make	made	made
break	broke	broken	mean	meant	meant
bring	brought	brought	meet	met	met
build	built	built	put	put	put
buy	bought	bought	quit	quit	quit
catch	caught	caught	read	read	read
choose	chose	chosen	ride	rode	ridden
come	came	come	ring	rang	rung
cost	cost	cost	rise	rose	risen
cut	cut	cut	run	ran	run
deal	dealt	dealt	say	said	said
do	did	done	see	saw	seen
draw	drew	drawn	sell	sold	sold
drink	drank	drunk	send	sent	sent
drive	drove	driven	set	set	set
eat	ate	eaten	shake	shook	shaken
fall	fell	fallen	shine	shone	shone
feed	fed	fed	shoot	shot	shot
feel	felt	felt	shut	shut	shut
fight	fought	fought	sing	sang	sung
find	found	found	sit	sat	sat
fly	flew	flown	sleep	slept	slept
forget	forgot	forgotten	speak	spoke	spoken
get	got	got/gotten	spend	spent	spent
give	gave	given	stand	stood	stood
go	went	gone	steal	stole	stolen
grow	grew	grown	strike	struck	struck
hang	hung	hung	swim	swam	swum
have	had	had	take	took	taken
hear	heard	heard	teach	taught	taught
hide	hid	hidden	tear	tore	torn
hit	hit	hit	tell	told	told
hold	held	held	think	thought	thought
hurt	hurt	hurt	throw	threw	thrown
keep	kept	kept	understand	understood	understood
know	knew	known	wake	waked/woke	waked/woken
lay	laid	laid	wear	wore	worn
lead	led	led	win	won	won
leave	left	left	write	wrote	written

PRESENT PARTICIPLES

aching	daring	flattering	promising
amazing	depressing	frightening	relaxing
amusing	deserving	frustrating	satisfying
annoying	disappointing	horrifying	shocking
appealing	disgusting	inspiring	surprising
astonishing	embarrassing	interesting	terrifying
boring	encouraging	inviting	tiring
changing	entertaining	irritating	troubling
charming	exciting	lasting	understanding
confusing	fascinating	pleasing	upsetting
convincing			

PAST PARTICIPLES

amazed	disappointed	horrified	satisfied
amused	disgusted	hurt	scared
annoyed	distinguished	improved	shocked
ashamed	embarrassed	injured	surprised
astonished	excited	inspired	terrified
bored	favored	interested	tired
broken	forgotten	pleased	troubled
complicated	frightened	protected	upset
confused	frustrated	qualified	wasted
depressed	hidden	relaxed	worried
dignified			

ask out = invite someone to do something (go to a show, a meal)
He asked her out to a movie.

be against = oppose
I'm against building a toy factory in City Park.

be back = return
I'm going to the drugstore. I'll be back in fifteen minutes.

be fed up with = be completely bored
I'm fed up with working. I want to have some fun.

be over = be finished
The meeting will be over in a few minutes.

break into = enter illegally, especially by force (a bank, building, house, etc.)
Last month a burglar broke into my apartment and took the TV.

bring up = mention or introduce a subject
You can bring up the question of child care at the next meeting.

call off = cancel (an event, arrangement, activity)
We had to call off the picnic because of rain.

catch up with = reach (someone who is ahead)
He was walking fast. I had to run to catch up with him.

cheer up = become happier
My sister was feeling depressed, but she cheered up when you invited her to the party.

come up with = think of, produce (an idea, plan, suggestion)
We must come up with a plan to improve the economy.

count on = depend on, rely on (someone)
If you ever need help, you can always count on me.

do without = manage in the absence of a person or thing
I like coffee, but I can do without it.

feel up to = feel strong enough (to do something)
I'm very tired. I don't feel up to playing tennis.

figure out = understand (someone or something) with difficulty
I can't figure out why she married Bill. He has nothing to offer.

fill in = complete (a form, questionnaire)
It took me fifteen minutes to fill in the application form.

find out = discover after making an effort
How did you find out that she was living in Paris?

get away = escape, be free to leave
The police chased the bandit, but he got away.

get away with = do something wrong or illegal without being punished
She always cheats on her exams. I don't know how she gets away with it.

get back = reach home again
We spent the whole day at the beach and didn't get back until after dark.

get over = recover from (an illness, a shock, a disappointment)
I had the flu last week, but I got over it quickly.

get through = finish, complete (some work, a job, a book)
She had a lot of work to do yesterday, but she got through all of it.

give in = stop resisting, surrender
Her boyfriend didn't want to go dancing, but he finally gave in.

give up = stop trying to do something (often because it is too difficult)
He tried to pick some oranges, but he couldn't reach them. So, he gave up.

go ahead = proceed, continue
Go ahead. Don't wait for me.

go away = leave, leave this place
Go away! I don't want to see you!

go on = continue any action
Go on with your story. It's very interesting.

go out = go to a social event (as to go to a theater, concert)
She has a lot of friends and goes out a lot.

grow up = become adult
Children grow up very fast nowadays.

hold on = wait (especially on the telephone)
Hold on. I'll be with you in a minute.

hold up = rob
Two gunmen held up the National Bank last week.

leave out = omit
When he filled out the application form, he left out his phone number.

let someone down = disappoint someone (often by breaking a promise or agreement)
You let me down. You promised to help me, but you didn't.

look after = take care of (someone or something)
My neighbor looks after the dog while I'm away.

look forward to = expect with pleasure
We're looking forward to the party next week.

look someone up = visit someone
She looked up her uncle when she was in San Francisco.

look up to = respect, admire
People look up to Dr. Pasto because of his great knowledge.

make up for = compensate for (a mistake, doing or not doing something)
I'm sorry I forgot your birthday, but I'll make it up to you.

move out = leave a house or apartment with one's possessions
Our neighbors moved out of their apartment yesterday.

pick up = get, collect (something or someone)
She picked up a package at the post office.

pick up = give someone a ride in a vehicle
He picked up his girlfriend after work and drove her home.

point out = show, explain
She pointed out that a small car is more practical than a big car.

put off = delay or postpone (doing something until a later time)
Never put off until tomorrow what you can do today.

put something back = return, replace (something)
When you finish looking at the magazines, put them back on the shelf.

put up with = suffer, tolerate (a difficult situation or person)
Our neighbors make a lot of noise, and we have to put up with it.

run into = meet someone by chance
I was on my way home when I ran into an old friend.

run out of = use all of and have none left (money, time, patience)
She ran out of money and had to borrow some from me.

see about = make inquiries or arrangements
We called the travel agency to see about getting a flight to New York.

see off = say good-bye to someone who is going on a trip
I saw my brother off at the airport last Sunday.

stand up for = defend verbally
Her mother criticized her, but her father stood up for her.

take off = remove an article of clothing
It was very hot, so he took off his coat.

take over = become the person or group in charge
He took over the business after his father died.

take up = begin (a hobby, sport, or kind of study)
Last year she took up stamp collecting, and now it's her favorite pastime.

talk over = discuss a matter with someone else
Whenever he has a problem, he talks it over with his wife.

think over = consider carefully (a problem, offer, situation)
You don't have to make a decision right away. Go home and think it over.

try on = put on (an article of clothing) to see how it fits
She tried on several dresses before finding one she liked.

try out = test
You should try out the computer before buying it.

turn down = refuse, reject (an offer, an application, an applicant)
He applied for a job at the bank but was turned down.

turn out = result, develop, or end
Don't worry. Everything will turn out all right.

turn up/down = increase/decrease (volume, force, pressure)
Would you please turn down the radio? It's too loud.

wear out = use (something) until it is finished
He has worn out three pairs of shoes in the last year.

work out = find the solution to a problem
We don't have enough money to pay all our expenses, but we'll work things out somehow.

VERBS FOLLOWED BY GERUND

Subject	Verb	Gerund	
They	enjoyed	watching	the football game.

admit	dislike	mind	remember
avoid	enjoy	miss	risk
consider	finish	postpone	save
debate	imagine	practice	stop
delay	keep	protest	suggest
discuss	mention	recommend	

VERBS FOLLOWED BY INFINITIVE OR GERUND

Subject	Verb	Infinitive/Gerund	
She	likes	to swim / swimming	in the ocean.

attempt	deserve	like	remember
begin	forget	love	start
bother	hate	prefer	try
continue	intend	regret	

VERBS FOLLOWED BY OBJECT + INFINITIVE (with **TO**)

Subject	Verb	Object	Infinitive (with To)	
I	wanted	him	to clean	the windows.

advise	choose	get	need	teach
allow	convince	help	order	tell
ask	encourage	hire	pay	train
beg	expect	inspire	remind	want
cause	force	invite	send	warn

GERUNDS

VERB AND PREPOSITION FOLLOWED BY GERUND

Subject	Verb + Preposition	Gerund	
We	believe in	helping	our friends.

admit to	care about	forget about	pay for
apologize for	complain about	insist on	plan on
approve of	count on	laugh about	succeed in
argue about	decide against	lie about	talk about/of
ask about	dream about/of	look forward to	think about/of
believe in	feel like	object to	worry about

ADJECTIVE AND PREPOSITION FOLLOWED BY GERUND

Subject	Be	Adjective + Preposition	Gerund	
He	is	afraid of	losing	his job.

accustomed to	disappointed about	interested in	sorry about/for
afraid of	disturbed about	lucky at	surprised at/about
ashamed of	excited about	new at	tired of
bad at	famous for	opposed to	upset about/over
bored with	fast at	proud of	used to
capable of	fond of	responsible for	worried about
careful about	glad about	sad about	
concerned about/with	good at	sick of	
confident of	happy about	slow at	

TAPESCRIPT FOR PAGE 15

ELLEN: I never have any fun. Every day I go to work, do my job, and go home. What a life!

ROBERT: Ellen's really something. I'd like to ask her for a date. But she probably wouldn't be interested in a guy like me.

TAPESCRIPT FOR PAGE 35

FRANCO FELLINI: Go to the table.
Sit down.
Pick up the letter.
Read the letter.
Throw the letter in the wastebasket.
Get up and leave the room.

TAPESCRIPT FOR PAGE 54

LISTENING

MR. BASCOMB: Mrs. Warbucks, I need money for my campaign. It's very important. Will you make a contribution?

MRS. WARBUCKS: I haven't decided yet. I want to know more about your plans for Wickam City.

PAIR WORK

ANTONIO: Darling, I love you. More than anything.

ULA HACKEY: Oh, Antonio. I love you, too.

ANTONIO: Marry me. We can live in Spain. We'll be very happy.

ULA HACKEY: But . . . how can I leave my career? I'm a movie star.

ANTONIO: You can learn Spanish and make movies in Spain.

ULA HACKEY: Antonio, you're asking too much.

MR. PENFIELD: Miss Hackey, I've been hearing rumors about a special man in your life. Is it true? Do you have a new boyfriend?

ULA HACKEY: Yes. His name's Antonio. He's from Spain.

MR. PENFIELD: Have you ever been to Spain?

ULA HACKEY: No, I haven't. Not yet.

MR. PENFIELD: Can you speak Spanish?

ULA HACKEY: *Un poquito.*

MR. PENFIELD: How long have you known Antonio?

ULA HACKEY: Six weeks.

MR. PENFIELD: How did you meet him?

ULA HACKEY: At a fabulous party in San Francisco.

MR. PENFIELD: Is Antonio romantic?

ULA HACKEY: Very.

MR. PENFIELD: Are you in love?

ULA HACKEY: (she giggles)

MR. PENFIELD: Are there wedding bells in your future?

ULA HACKEY: I really can't say.

MR. PENFIELD: Why won't you tell me?

ULA HACKEY: It's too soon.

MR. PENFIELD: Well, I wish you and Antonio all the best.

ULA HACKEY: Thanks, Wilder. Bye-bye.

1.

BRUNO: Nick's Garage. Bruno speaking.

GLORIA: I'm calling about the car you have for sale.

BRUNO: You mean the Pontiac?

GLORIA: Yes. Is it in good condition?

BRUNO: Yes, ma'am. Drove it myself.

GLORIA: How much are you asking for it?

BRUNO: Four thousand dollars.

GLORIA: I'd like to see the car.

BRUNO: Sure. We're open 'til five.

GLORIA: Thank you.

2.

MS. DUNSON: Good morning. Sunshine Travel. May I help you?

MR. FARLEY: I want to get some information. Can you recommend a good place for a relaxing vacation?

MS. DUNSON: Sure. I have just the place. It's called Paradise Island.

MR. FARLEY: Paradise . . . that sounds good. Where is it?

MS. DUNSON: The South Pacific. Shall I send you a brochure?

MR. FARLEY: Yes, please do.

3.

RICHARD: Foursquare Appliances. Richard speaking.

GLADYS: I'm calling about the fan you sold me.

RICHARD: What's the problem?

GLADYS: It doesn't work.

RICHARD: Doesn't work?

GLADYS: Yeah. I plugged it in and nothing happened.

RICHARD: Okay, bring it in and I'll take a look at it.

GLADYS: I'll be right over.

4.

MS. SANDERS: Golden Opportunity Employment Company. May I help you?

MR. RIPKEN: I'm looking for a job in sales. My name's Al Ripken.

MS. SANDERS: Do you have any experience?

MR. RIPKEN: Eighteen years.

MS. SANDERS: Good. I'm sure we can help you. Would you like to schedule an appointment?

MR. RIPKEN: How about tomorrow?

MS. SANDERS: Let's see . . . there's an opening at ten.

MR. RIPKEN: Fine. See you at ten.

5.

BLOSSOM: Bedford Arms. May I help you?

CARLOS: I'm calling about the apartment you have for rent.

BLOSSOM: It's still available.

CARLOS: I need a quiet place.

BLOSSOM: It's very quiet. Come and see for yourself.

CARLOS: How about this afternoon?

BLOSSOM: That'll be fine.

6.

STANLEY: Ace Plumbing. Can I help you?

MRS. GOLO: My kitchen drain is stopped up!

STANLEY: No problem. We're the drain-cleaning experts.

MRS. GOLO: How much do you charge?

STANLEY: A hundred dollars, more or less.

MRS. GOLO: Can you come today?

STANLEY: No, we're very busy. I can send someone Friday.

MRS. GOLO: I can't wait that long!

1. **MR. BASCOMB:** I'd love to take you dancing, but I have a headache.

   MRS. BASCOMB: That's what you always say!

2. **SALESMAN:** This baby runs like new!

   CUSTOMER: Oh, really? I can't wait to take her for a drive.

3. **JENNY:** The dog ate my homework.

   MRS. GOLO: Oh, sure.

4. **LUISA:** It's delicious!

   CARLOS: I'm glad you like it.

5. **HONEST JOHN:** I promise to build more schools, more hospitals, more of everything. And I'll lower your taxes . . . all at the same time!

   AUDIENCE: (applause and cheers)

6. **YOUNG WOMAN:** I love you for yourself. I don't care about your money.

   OLD MAN: Mmmm hmmm.